Wicca
Candle
Magick

Wicca
Candle
Magick

By Gerina Dunwich

A Citadel Press Book
Published by Carol Publishing Group

Carol Publishing Group Edition, 1997

Previously published as *The Magick of Candle Burning.*

A Citadel Press Book
Published by Carol Publishing Group
Citadel Press is a registered trademark of Carol Communications, Inc.

Editorial, sales and distribution, rights and permissions inquiries
should be addressed to Carol Publishing Group, 120 Enterprise Avenue,
Secaucus, N.J. 07094

In Canada: Canadian Manda Group, One Atlantic Avenue, Suite 105,
Toronto, Ontario M6K 3E7

Carol Publishing Group books may be purchased in bulk at special
discounts for sales promotions, fund-raising, or educational purposes.
Special editions can be created to specifications. For details, contact
Special Sales Department, Carol Publishing Group, 120 Enterprise Avenue,
Secaucus, N.J. 07094

Manufactured in the United States of America
10 9 8 7 6 5 4 3

Library of Congress Cataloging-in-Publication Data

Dunwich, Gerina.
  [Magick of candle burning.]
  Wicca candle magick / Gerina Dunwich.
        p.   cm.
  "A Citadel Press book."
  Previously published: The magick of candle burning. 1989.
  Includes index.
  ISBN 0-8065-1831-6
  1. Candles and lights—Miscellanea. 2. Magic. I. Title.
[BF1623.C26D86   1996]
133.4'3—dc20   96-33388
                                                        CIP

I dedicate this book with loving gratitude to my Mother and Al Jackter for giving me encouragement and spiritual support. I would also like to thank Jessica Black for all of her assistance, and Bob Salomon for helping to make this book possible.

Contents

Introduction: The Magick of Candles   13
1. Candle Crafting.   17
2. Consecration   25
3. Symbolism of Candle Colors   31
4. Candle Magick for Healing.   59
5. Sabbat Candle Rituals   89
6. Candle Magick 123
7. Magick for Hearth and Home 151
8. Voudoun Candle Magick 159
9. Candle Omens and Superstitions 175
10. Resources 181
Index 192

The Magick of Candles

The soft, mellow glow of candlelight creates romantic moods, invokes spirits and utilizes the ancient element of Fire, which is known as the sacred element of magickal transformation.

The dancing flame of a candle gives off mystical power and has been used for centuries by Witches and magicians as a tool for setting the proper atmosphere or spellcasting, divination and meditation, banishing darkness, and as a means of communicating with the dead. The symbolism of creating light in darkness also lies behind the use of the candle in rituals of magick.

The candle is also an image of humanity. The wax of the candle corresponds to the physical body; the wick corresponds to the mind, and the flame corresponds to the spirit or soul.

Candles come in all different sizes, shapes and colors, and can be bought in candle shops, gift shops, occult shops and Witchcraft supply mail order catalogues (see Chapter Ten: Resources); however, many Witches and magicians prefer to work magick with their own home-made candles rather than store bought ones for it is believed that hand-crafted candles with pentagrams and/or other magickal symbols and sigils cut into the wax are more magickally powerful than mass-produced ones since they absorb the Witch's or magician's own psychic energies. (The ancient craft of candlemaking is discussed in Chapter One.)

Candle colors are very important when it comes to performing magick, for each color emits a special vibration and attracts different spiritual influences. (See Chapter Three for the symbolism of candle colors.)

The shape that the candle is fashioned in also possesses significance in candleburning magick. Black cat-shaped candles are burned in magick spells to increase luck and psychic power. White cat-shaped candles are burned to make wishes come true and to protect pregnant women. Moon-shaped candles (or candles decorated with lunar symbols) are burned to add power to moon-magick and Goddess invocations. Human image candles made in both male and female figures are used to represent the man or woman whom the power of a spell is directed at. Phallic-shaped candles are powerful when used in fertility rites and sex-magick. Mummy-shaped candles, which are difficult to obtain, are burned in spells to acquire power and success and to invoke ancient Egyptian deities. Devil-shaped candles are used in both black and white magick Voodoo spells. Black skull-shaped candles are burned to cast or reverse hexes, and in rituals of separation. White skull-shaped candles are used in healing rituals and seances. Seven-

Knob candles, which consist of seven balls of wax strung together with one wick, are burned as daily meditation candles or as wish-magick candles with each segment of the candle burned daily as the wish to be granted is concentrated upon.

Candle-gazing, or fire-scrying, is a form of divination practiced by Witches, Gypsies and seers long before candles first became popular in Europe in the Middle Ages.

To divine using a candle, clear your mind and then gaze into the flame of the candle until you enter a trance-like state in which images, symbols, people or words will begin to appear as part of a psychic communication.

> *THE GODDESS IS ALIVE*
> *MAGICK IS AFOOT*
> *BLESSED BE!*

1

Candle Crafting

Witch Candles

To make homemade Witch Candles, you will need the following items which are obtainable at most hobby and craft stores as well as candle shops: candle wicking, wick tins, fireproof candle molds, wire rods, equal parts paraffin and pure beeswax (amounts depending upon how many candles are to be crafted) and a double boiler for melting the wax.

Place the end of a metal core wick (pre-cut to fit the size of the mold and allowing at least one extra inch of wick above the top of the mold) through the star-cut stamped in the center of a wick tin and then bend the tips of the star down to hold the wick in place.

Place the wick tin and wick in a candle mold with the wick centered by a loop in a wire rod placed across the top of the mold. (Candle molds, plain and fancy, are also available in most of the shops that sell crafts and candles. Ordinary household things such as empty waxed milk cartons, plastic bottles, paper towel rolls, paper cups and metal cans make wonderful molds that are inexpensive and disposable.)

Non-disposable candle molds such as muffin cups and fireproof tumblers can be made stick-proof with special candle spray, silicone sprays or non-stick sprays for frying pans. Another (and more old-fashioned) method to prevent candles from sticking to the molds is to grease and then dust the mold with flour or talcum powder.

Cut the paraffin into small pieces with a sharp knife and place them inside the top of the double boiler. (A large tin can placed in a pan of boiling water may be used in place of the double boiler.) Partially fill the bottom part of the boiler with warm water and then place the top part with the cut-up wax inside of it. Add the beeswax to the paraffin and place the double boiler over low heat to melt the wax. (Never attempt to melt the wax directly over fire!)

Scent the melted wax with an aromatic herb oil appropriate for the type of magick spell the candle will be used for. For instance, scent the candle wax with oil of cloves if the candle will be used for divination, exorcism or rituals involving spiritual purification; frankincense oil for love spells, consecration, healing, protection and rituals to banish evil and negativity; lavender oil for love spells; lemon oil for healing rituals and spells involving clairvoyance and prophetic dreams; mint oil for exorcism and healing rituals; musk oil for love spells, sex-magick and fertility rites; patchouly oil for love spells and invocations of elemental powers; pine oil for spells to attract money and success; rose oil for Goddess invocations and spells to increase good luck, courage and love; sandalwood oil for purification rites, healing and protection against evil influences.

To make colored candles, melt a colored wax crayon in the paraffin. (See Chapter Three for the symbolism of candle colors.)

After the melted wax has been scented and colored, remove the double boiler from the heat and slowly pour the wax into the mold(s). Allow it to solidify.

After the wax has cooled, a conical cavity may form on the top surface around the wick. Pour enough melted wax to fill the cavity and provide a level surface to the candle.

Remove the candle from the mold only after the wax has cooled and hardened thoroughly.

Before burning the candle in a magickal ceremony, anoint it with a small amount of oil to put your psychic vibrations into the candle, magnetize it and transform it into an extension of your mind power. (See Chapter Two: Consecration.)

Beeswax Candles

Beeswax candles are tapers fashioned from the honeycombs of bees and used in special magickal spells and rituals that require that no tallow (animal fat) be burned.

To make beeswax candles, wrap or roll a honeycomb sheet of beeswax around a candle wick. (Artificial honeycombs of beeswax are obtainable from beekeepers, waxchandlers, honey wholesalers and hobby shops.)

Cut the wax sheet to the size you desire. (For a 6-inch long candle, cut a 12-inch wax sheet in half.)

Place the wax on a smooth surface. Press the wick vertically against the shorter side of the wax sheet and begin to roll the sheet around the wick. (If the wax is cut on top at a slanting angle away from the wick, the candle's shape will be enhanced by its tapering conical contour.)

Anoint the candle with oil to consecrate it and charge it with power before using it in spells or magickal ceremonies.

Rune Candles

Runes are letters of magickal alphabets used to spell words containing powerful mystic meanings. There are many different forms of Runes, including the Druidic Ogam Bethluisnion, Egyptian hieroglyphics, Theban Script, Pictish, Celestial, Malachim, etc.

To make Rune Candles, heat the tip of a consecrated athame and use it to carve the magickal designs into the wax of smooth tapers or jumbo candles. (A heated steel knitting needle or nail can also be used just as effectively.)

Magick Symbol Candles

Other powerful Pagan symbols that can be carved into (or painted on) candles include the sign of the *Pentagram* (a five-pointed star within a circle) which represents the four ancient elements of Fire, Water, Air, Earth, surmounted by the Spirit, and is used in many spells and magickal ceremonies.

As a Witch's Star (or "Goblin's Cross" as it was called by churchmen of the Middle Ages), the pentagram symbolizes human spiritual aspirations when its point faces upwards. When its point faces down, it becomes a negative symbol of black magick and Satanism.

The *Crescent Moon* is a sacred symbol of the Goddess and feminine energy. It is the appropriate symbol to be used on candles crafted especially for Goddess invocations, Sabbats and women's healing.

The ancient magickal symbol called the *Seal of Solomon* is a hexagram consisting of two interlocking triangles, one facing up and the other one facing down. It is a symbol of the human soul, and is most powerful when used on candles crafted for spells and rituals involving spirit communication, wisdom, purification and the strengthening of psychic powers.

The *ankh* is an ancient Egyptian symbol resembling a cross with a loop at the top. It symbolizes life and cosmic knowledge, and every major god and goddess of the Egyptian mythology is depicted carrying it. Also known as the "crux ansata," it is an appropriate symbol to place on candles for spells and rituals involving health, fertility and divination.

The *Eye of Horus* is another ancient Egyptian symbol which is often used in contemporary Witchcraft. It depicts the divine eye of the god Horus, represents both solar and lunar energies, and is carved into candles to symbolize spiritual protection as well as the clairvoyant power of the Third Eye.

The *triangle* is a symbol of finite manifestation in Western magick, and is used in rituals to evoke spirits when the seal or sign of the entity to be summoned is placed in the center of the triangle.

Triangles containing veves (intricate symbolic emblems representing certain Voodoo spirit-loas) are extremely powerful when carved into candles. (See Chapter Nine: Voudoun Candle Magick.)

The triangle, equivalent to the number three (a powerful magickal number) is also a symbol of the Triple Goddess: Mother, Warrior, Crone. Inverted, it represents the male principle.

The *Swastika* is an ancient religious symbol formed by a Greek cross with the ends of the arms bent at right angles in either a clockwise or counterclockwise direction. Before being adopted in 1935 as the infamous official emblem of Nazi Germany, the Swastika was a sacred symbol of good luck in pre-Christian Pagan Europe and in many other cultures around the world including the Orientals, the Egyptians and the Indian tribes of North, Central and South America. (The word "Swastika" stems from the Sanskrit "Svastika" meaning "a sign of good luck.")

In addition to the above-mentioned symbols of magick, there are numerous ancient as well as modern mystical symbols that can be used to empower candles with specific magickal energies. These symbols include the male and female fertility symbols, crosses, circles, peace signs, astrological and planetary symbols, numbers, etc.

2

Consecration

Before using any candle (hand-made or store-bought) in a magickal ceremony or in the simplest of spells, it is recommended that you first dress (anoint) the candle with a small amount of oil during the waxing phase of the moon to consecrate it and charge it with magickal energy.

Candle Blessing Ritual

Using your bare hands, rub an anointing oil into the wax starting at the middle of the candle and working your way up to the top as you say:

> I CONSECRATE THEE
> AS A TOOL OF MAGICK.
> BLESSED BE!

Start again at the middle and this time work your way down tc the bottom of the candle and say:

> I CHARGE THEE WITH POWER
> IN THE NAME OF THE GODDESS.
> SO MOTE IT BE!

GODDESS OIL

½ teaspoon dried yarrow
½ teaspoon dried sweet basil
1 teaspoon powdered myrrh
3 drops rose oil
3 drops lavender oil
½ cup olive oil

Place all ingredients in a clear glass jar and gently swirl in a clockwise direction to slowly agitate the oils. (As you do this, fill your mind with images of the Goddess and visualize Her divine power as an aura of white glowing light radiating from your hands into the jar of oil, charging it with magickal energy.)

Seal the jar with a tight-fitting lid and store it in a cool, dark place for at least seven days. Strain the oil through a cheesecloth and use it to anoint candles for love spells, Goddess invocations, divinations, healing rituals and all positive (white) forms of magick.

GOOD LUCK OIL

1 tablespoon dried wormwood
3 teaspoons ground nutmeg
½ teaspoon powdered mandrake root
13 drops pine oil
¼ cup olive oil

Place all ingredients in a clean glass jar and gently swirl in a clockwise direction. Seal the jar tightly and allow it to sit for 13 nights in a cool, dark place.

Strain the oil through a cheesecloth and use it to anoint candles for wish-magick, jinx-breaking and spells to attract good luck, money and success.

SPIRIT OIL

1 tablespoon powdered orris or serpentaria root
1 tablespoon dried Solomon's Seal
1 tablespoon dried and crushed rosemary
1 small pinch of powdered jade or turquoise*
3 drops sandalwood oil
3 drops mint oil
¼ cup safflower oil

Mix all of the ingredients together and store in a tightly-capped glass jar for at least three weeks in a cool, dark place.

Strain through a cheesecloth and use to anoint candles for exorcisms, seances, counterspells, purification rituals, protection against evil influences and spells to increase clairvoyant powers.

---

* Gemstones can be easily powdered using a metal file.

VOODOO-WITCH OIL

3 tablespoons honey
3 teaspoons powdered bat's skull (optional)
13 drops blood (human or animal)
6 drops honeysuckle oil
3 drops patchouly oil
¼ cup sunflower oil

Mix all of the ingredients together on a night of the full moon and use it to anoint Voodoo candles for both white and black magick spells, divination, spirit communication and invocation of loas.

3

Symbolism of Candle Colors

Magick Candle Colors

Before casting spells or performing any kind of magick, the color of the candle should be chosen carefully according to your purpose, for each color possesses a different energy vibration and attracts certain influences.

The following is a list of candle colors and their magickal properties:

BLACK: Meditation rituals, hexes, uncrossing rituals and spells to banish evil and negativity.

BLUE: Magick that involves honor, loyalty, peace, tranquility, truth, wisdom, protection during sleep, astral projection and spells to induce prophetic dreams.

BROWN: Spells to locate lost objects and improve powers of concentration and telepathy, protection of familiars and household pets.

GOLD: Spells that attract the power of cosmic influences, and rituals to honor solar deities.

GRAY: Spells to neutralize negative influences.

GREEN: Spells involving fertility, success, good luck, prosperity, money, rejuvenation and ambition, rituals to counteract greed and jealousy.

ORANGE: Spells to stimulate energy.

PINK: Love spells and rituals involving friendship and femininity.

PURPLE: Psychic manifestations, healing and spells involving power, success, independence and household protection.

RED: Fertility rites, aphrodisiacs and spells involving sexual passion, love, health, physical strength, revenge, anger, will power, courage and magnetism.

SILVER: Spells and rituals to remove negativity, encourage stability and attract the influence of the Goddess.

WHITE: Consecration rituals, meditation, divination, exorcism, and spells that involve healing, clairvoyance, truth, peace, spiritual strength and lunar energy.

YELLOW: Spells involving confidence, attraction, charm and persuasion.

Sabbat Candle Colors

CANDLEMAS: Red, pink, brown.
SPRING EQUINOX: Green, yellow, gold.
BELTANE: Dark green.
SUMMER SOLSTICE: Green, blue.
LAMMAS: Yellow, orange.
AUTUMN EQUINOX: Orange, brown, yellow.
SAMHAIN: Black, orange.
YULE: Red, green, white.

Zodiac Candle Colors

Each of the 12 astrological signs of the zodiac is ruled by its own color. It is important when casting horoscopes or performing zodiac-related magick that the colors of the candles used correspond to the proper zodiacal color:

ARIES: Red
TAURUS: Green
GEMINI: Yellow or silver
CANCER: White
LEO: Gold or yellow
VIRGO: Gray
LIBRA: Royal blue
SCORPIO: Black or red
SAGITTARIUS: Dark blue or purple
CAPRICORN: Black or dark brown
AQUARIUS: Light blue
PISCES: Aquamarine

Daily Colors

Each day of the week is ruled by its own magickal color. Candles used in daily meditation rituals should be of the following colors:

SUNDAY: Yellow
MONDAY: White
TUESDAY: Red
WEDNESDAY: Purple
THURSDAY: Blue
FRIDAY: Green
SATURDAY: Black

Sacred Candle Colors of the Gods and Goddesses

Just as Christianity is made up of many different religious denominations, there are many different traditions in Witchcraft (or Wicca, as many modern Witches prefer to call it). Each Wiccan tradition has different rituals and festivals, and many use a different name for the Goddess and Her consort, the Horned God.

Although white altar candles alone can usually be used to invoke the Pagan deities, using a special candle of the appropriate sacred color when invoking a particular God or Goddess will bring much better results.

The following alphabetical list contains the names, descriptions and sacred candle colors of most of the Goddesses and Gods worshipped by the various Wiccan traditions as well as many of the ancient nature deities honored by different Pagan cultures throughout history. (For the sacred candle colors of the Voodoo gods and goddesses [loas], see the list of Rada and Petro loas in Chapter Eight: Voudoun Candle Magick.)

AAH
One of the sacred Moon-Gods of ancient Egypt. His sacred candle color is silver.

ADITI
Hindu Sky-Goddess. Her sacred candle color is blue.

AGNI
Hindu god who takes three forms: the sun, lightning, and fire. His sacred candle color is red.

AMATERASU-O-MI-KAMI
Japanese Sun-Goddess. Her sacred candle colors are yellow and gold.

AMON (or Amen)
Egyptian god of life, reproduction and agriculture; represented as a man with a ram's head. His sacred candle color is green.

ANAITIS
Persian Fertility-Goddess. Her sacred candle color is green.

ANU
Celtic Mother-Goddess, Dawn-Mother, and Goddess of death and the dead. Her sacred candle colors are white and black.

ANUBIS
Egyptian god of death and black magick who appears in the form of a dog or as a man with the head of a jackal. In Egyptian mythology, he was the son of Nephthys, and at times he rivaled the great god Osiris in importance. His sacred candle color is black.

AODH
Celtic Fire-Goddess. Her sacred candle color is red.

APHRODITE
Greek goddess of love and beauty, and one of the Twelve Great Olympians. She is also known as Cytherea, and is identified with the Roman Love-Goddess Venus. Her sacred candle colors are red and pink.

APOLLO

Greek god of the sun, fertility, prophecy and oracles, and also a deity associated with light, healing, music and poetry. In Greek mythology, He was the son of Zeus, the twin brother of the Moon-Goddess Artemis, and one of the Twelve Great Olympians. His sacred candle colors are gold and white.

ARRIANRHOD

Welsh Mother-Goddess and Neo-Pagan goddess of fertility. Her sacred candle colors are green and white.

ARTEMIS

Greek goddess of the moon, hunting and wild beasts. As a lunar goddess, she has been an influential archetype for Witches and worshippers of the contemporary Goddess-cult. She is the equivalent of the Roman Moon-Goddess Diana, and is identified with Luna, Hecate and Selene. Her sacred candle colors are silver and white.

ASHERALI

Canaanite goddess of the moon and fertility. Her sacred candle colors are green, white and silver.

ASTARTE

Phoenician goddess of love and fertility. She is identified with the moon and depicted with crescent horns. Her sacred candle colors are pink, green, red and silver.

ASTRAEA

Greek goddess of innocence and purity, and daughter of Themis, the goddess of justice. It is said that after leaving Earth, she was placed among the stars where she became the constellation Virgo the Virgin. Her sacred candle color is white.

ATHENA

Greek goddess of wisdom and the arts, and one of the Twelve Great Olympians. She is identified with the Roman goddess Minerva, and her sacred candle colors are purple and white.

ATTIS

Phrypian god of fertility and vegetation, and consort of the Fertility-Goddess Cybele. His sacred candle color is green.

BAAL

Phoenician god of nature and fertility, associated with winter rain. He is depicted as a warrior with a horned helmet and spear, and was once worshipped as the principal god on earth for thousand of years. His sacred candle color is green.

BACCHUS

Roman god of wine and gaiety; identified with the Greek Wine-God Dionysus. In mythology, He was the son of the deities Zeus and Semele, and the consort of Ariadne. His sacred candle colors are red and purple.

BALDER

Scandinavian Sun-God, son of Odin, and the personification of wisdom, goodness and beauty. His sacred candle colors are yellow and gold.

BAST

Egyptian Fertility-Goddess and daughter of Isis, also known as the Lady of Light. She bestows health and symbolizes sexual passion. In ancient times, she was worshipped in the form of a cat. Later, she was envisaged as a woman with the head of a cat. Bast is one of the most popular ancient Egyptian Goddesses in modern day Witchcraft and sex-magick cults. Her sacred candle colors are red, green and white.

BENTEN
Japanese Buddhist Love-Goddess. She is also the goddess of femininity, music, literature and the sea. Her sacred candle color is pink.

BRIGIT
Celtic and Neo-Pagan goddess of fire, wisdom, poetry and sacred wells, and also a deity associated with prophecy, divination and healing. Her sacred candle colors are red and white.

CE-AEHD
Celtic goddess of nature. Her sacred candle color is green.

CEARA
Ancient Pagan goddess of nature and feminine equivalent to the god Cearas. Her sacred candle color is green.

CEARAS
Ancient Pagan god of fire and masculine equivalent to the goddess Ceara. His sacred candle color is red.

CENTEOTLE
Mexican Fertility-Goddess. Her sacred candle color is green.

CERES
Roman goddess of harvest and fertility of the earth, and mother of Proserpina. In Greek mythology, She is Demeter the goddess of agriculture, and mother of Persephone. Her sacred candle colors are green, orange, brown and yellow.

CERNUNNOS
Celtic horned nature-god of wild animals, hunting and fertility, "Lord of All Living Creatures," and consort of the Great Mother. He is depicted as having the head of a bull, the torso of a man, and the tail of a fish. As a Neo-Pagan god, he is worshipped mainly by Wiccans of the Gardnerian tradition. His sacred candle color is dark green.

CERRIDWEN
Celtic and Neo-Pagan goddess of mountains, fertility and inspiration. Her sacred candle color is green.

CHERNOBOG
Slavic god of storms and war, also known as the Thunderer and the Hurler of Lightning Bolts. His sacred candle color is red.

CHLORIS
Greek goddess of flowers, and equivalent of the Roman Flower-Goddess Flora. Her sacred candle colors are white and all floral colors.

CHU-JUNG
Chinese god of fire. His sacred candle color is red.

CYBELE
Phrygian goddess of nature and fertility, consort of the god Attis, and equivalent to the Greek Mother-Goddess Rhea. Cybele is symbolically associated with wild animals and mountains, and is represented in myth riding in a chariot drawn by lions. Her sacred candle color is green.

DAGHDA
Principal god of the Pagan tribes of Ireland, "Lord of Great Knowledge," and god of fertility and the earth. He was believed to control life and death with a great club and had a cauldron with magickal powers. His sacred candle colors are green and brown.

DAZHBOG
Slavic Sun-God and consort/brother of the goddess Zhiva. His sacred candle colors are yellow, gold and orange-red.

DEMETER
Greek goddess of fertility, husbandry and harvest, mother of Persephone, and an important deity in the mysteries of the Eleusis. She is identified with the Roman goddess Ceres, and her sacred candle colors are green and orange.

DEW
Greek Fertility-Goddess. Her sacred candle color is green.

DIANA
Roman and Neo-Pagan Moon-Goddess, Mother-Goddess and virgin huntress of the moon. She is identified with the Greek Lunar-Goddess Artemis and is wor-

shipped mainly by Wiccans of the Dianic tradition. Her sacred candle colors are silver and white.

DIONYSUS

Greek god of wine, ecstasy, fertility and nature, who was worshipped in frenzied orgies. He symbolizes freedom and spontaneous impulses, and is the equivalent of the Roman Wine-God Bacchus. His sacred candle colors are red, purple and green.

DURGA (also Durva)

Hindu goddess and consort of the god Shiva who was worshipped throughout India, but especially in Bengal. Durga is depicted as a ferocious ten-armed dragon-slayer, but it is said she is loving and gentle to those who worship her. Her sacred candle color is red.

DYAUS

Indo-European Sky-God, consort of the Earth-Goddess Prithivi, and father of Indra. His sacred candle color is blue.

EA

Babylonian god of water, lord of wisdom and patron of magick, arts and crafts; identified with the Sumerian god Enk. It is believed that the symbolism of the astrological sign of Capricorn derives from Ea as he is depicted as having the body of a goat and the tail of a fish. His sacred candle color is blue.

EOSTRE

Saxon and Neo-Pagan goddess of fertility and springtime, whom the holiday of Easter is named after. Her sacred candle color is green.

EPONA
Celtic Mare-Goddess whose sacred candle color is white.

ERESHKIGAL
Sumerian Horned-Goddess and Queen of the Under-world. She is identified with the Greek Lunar-Goddess Hecate, and depicted as having the body of a fish with serpent-like scales and the ears of a sheep. Her sacred candle color is black.

EROS
Greek god of love and sexual intercourse, the myth-ological son of Zeus and Aphrodite, and the personi-fication of universal passion. He is identified with Cu-pid, the Roman god of love and son of Venus. His sacred candle color is red.

ESMERALDA
South American goddess of love. Her sacred candle color is, of course, emerald green.

EXU
Macumba god of magick. His sacred candle colors are white and black.

FAUNUS
Roman god of woodlands, fields and shepherds. He is depicted as half-goat and half-human, and is the equiv-alent of the Greek Nature-God Pan. His sacred candle color is green.

FLORA
Roman goddess of flowers and "all that flourishes." She is the equivalent of the Greek Flower-Goddess Chloris,

and her sacred candle colors are white and all floral colors.

FORTUNA

Roman goddess of happiness, good fortune and chance who possesses the power to bestow upon mortals either wealth or poverty. She is identified with the Greek goddess Tyche, and her sacred candle colors are green, gold and silver.

FREY

Scandinavian god of fertility, who is appropriately represented with an erect phallus indicating his fertilizing power. He is also a deity associated with peace and prosperity. In Scandinavian mythology, he is the brother and consort of the goddess Freya, and the son of the sea-god Njord. His sacred candle color is green.

FREYA (also Freyja)

Scandinavian goddess of fertility, love and beauty, whose sacred symbols and familiars were cats. She is represented in myth as a beautiful woman riding in a golden chariot drawn by cats. She was also a Queen of the Underworld, and the sister and consort of the god Frey. As a Neo-Pagan goddess, she is worshipped mainly by Wiccans of the Saxon tradition. Her sacred candle colors are green, red and black.

FRIGGA

Scandinavian Mother-Goddess and consort of the god Odin. She is also the patroness of marriage and fecundity, and is represented in myth riding in a chariot drawn by sacred rams. Her sacred candle color is white.

FRIJA
Pagan-Germanic Earth-Mother and consort of the god Tiwaz. The day of the week sacred to her is Friday. Her sacred candle color is brown.

HADES
Greek god of the Underworld, ruler of the dead and brother of the mighty god Zeus. He is also known as Aidoneus, and in Roman mythology he is called Pluto. His sacred candle color is black.

HATHOR
Egyptian goddess of beauty and the heavens, and patroness of fecundity, infants and music. She is often depicted as a woman with a cow's head, wearing the head-dress of two plumes and a solar disc decorated with stars symbolizing Her role as a Sky-Goddess. Her sacred candle color is blue.

HECATE
Greek Moon-Goddess, Neo-Pagan goddess of fertility and moon-magick, Queen of the Underworld, and protectress of all Witches. She is also known as both the "Goddess of Darkness and Death" and the "Queen of Ghosts and Crossroads," and is identified with the lunar-goddess Diana and the Greek goddess Persephone. Her sacred candle colors are black and silver.

HERA
Greek goddess of death and rebirth, Earth-Goddess, and consort of the god Zeus. Her sacred candle colors are black and dark brown.

HESTIA
Greek Hearth-Goddess. Her sacred candle color is red.

HORUS
Egyptian god of the sky and son of Isis and Osiris. He is depicted as a falcon-headed man with the sun and moon as his eyes. His sacred candle color is royal blue.

INANNA
Sumerian goddess of both love and war, who is identified with the Babylonian goddess Ishtar. Her sacred candle color is red.

ISHTAR
Asyrian, Babylonian and Neo-Pagan goddess of love, fertility and war, who personifies the planet Venus. She was a Mother-Goddess and the consort of Tammuz, the god of grain and bread who died each winter and was reborn the following spring. As a Triple Goddess, she represents birth, death and rebirth. In her aspect as Mother, she is the giver of all life. In her aspect as Warrior-Maiden, she is the bringer of death. In her aspect as Crone, she brings rebirth and resurrection. The crescent of the new moon rising is one of Her sacred symbols and she is depicted as a woman with bird-like facial features and braided hair, wearing bull's horns and jeweled necklaces, bracelets and anklets. She is associated with the Sumerian goddess Inanna and the Phoenician goddess Astarte. Her sacred candle colors are red and green.

ISIS
Ancient Egyptian Mother-Goddess of fertility and Neo-Pagan goddess of magick and enchantment. She was the sister and consort of the Sun-God Osiris, and was at

times identified with the goddess Hathor. Isis is the symbol of divine motherhood, and she was regarded in Her Mysteries as the single form of all gods and goddesses. She is often called the "Goddess of Ten Thousand Names" and in Hellespont (now Dardanelles) she was known as Mystis, the Lady of the Mysteries. Her sacred candle color is green.

JANUS
Roman god of gates and doorways and a deity associated with journeys and the beginning of things. He is depicted as having two faces, each looking in opposite directions. His festival month was January and his sacred candle color is white.

KALI
Hindu Death-Goddess, personifying the dark and terrifying forces of nature. She is depicted as a fanged, dark-skinned warrior-like woman wearing a necklace of human skulls around her neck. Her sacred candle color is black.

KHONS
One of the sacred Moon-Gods of ancient Egypt. He was also known as a god of healing, and his sacred candle colors are silver and white.

KILYA
Inca Moon-Goddess. Her sacred candle colors are silver and white.

KUAN YIN
Chinese goddess of fertility, childbirth and compassion. Her sacred candle color is green.

KUPALA
Slavic goddess of life, sex and vitality. She is worshipped on Midsummer's Day, and her sacred candle color is red.

LOKI
Scandinavian god of fire. His sacred candle color is red.

LUCINA
Roman goddess of the moon who is also associated with childbirth. Her sacred candle colors are silver and white.

LUGH
Early Celtic Sun-God worshipped by the ancient Druids as the Bountiful Giver of Harvest. The pagan Sabbat festival of Lughnasadh (meaning "Commemoration of Lugh") was originated by the Druids to pay homage to the Sun-God. His sacred candle colors are yellow, gold and bronze.

LUNA
Roman and Neo-Pagan Moon-Goddess, whose name is Latin for "moon." She is identified with Selene and Artemis, and her sacred candle colors are white and silver.

LUPERCUS
Roman god of fertility, identified with the nature-gods Pan and Faunus. In ancient Rome, his fertility festival was celebrated as Lupercalia on February 15th. His sacred candle color is green.

MAAT
Egyptian goddess of truth, justice and the order of the universe, whose symbol was a feather. Her sacred candle color is white.

MIN
Egyptian god of fertility and protector of travelers. His sacred candle colors are green and white.

MORRIGAN
Celtic War-Goddess of death and destruction and the mother of all Irish gods. She is said to appear in the form of a raven (a bird of ill-omen in the Celtic tradition) before and during battles. She is also known as the "Spectre Queen" and "Great Queen Morgan." As a Goddess Trinity, she was called Macha when she worked magick with the blood of the slain; Badb when she appeared in the form of a giantess on the eve of war to warn soldiers of their fates, and Neman when she appeared as a shape-shifting crone. Her sacred candle colors are scarlet and black.

MUT
Egyptian goddess of fertility. Her sacred candle color is green.

MYLITTA
Babylonian goddess of fertility. Her sacred candle color is green.

NEMESIS
Greek goddess of anger and vengeance and mythological daughter of Erebus and Nyx. Her sacred candle color is red.

NEPTUNE
Roman god of the sea, brother of Zeus and equivalent of the Greek Sea-God Poseidon. His sacred candle color is blue.

NINHURSAG
Mesopotamian Earth-Goddess and consort of Ea. Her sacred candle color is dark brown.

NJORD
Scandinavian god of the sea and patron of fisherman. He is also known as the god of prosperity, and his sacred candle color is aquamarine.

NUT (also Nuit)
Egyptian Sky-Goddess and mother of Osiris, Isis, Set and Nephthys. Her sacred candle color is royal blue.

NYX
Greek goddess of night and both sister and consort of Erebus, the lord of darkness. She is identified with the Roman goddess Nox. Her sacred candle color is black.

ODIN
Scandinavian and Neo-Pagan god of wisdom, magick, art and poetry. He is also the Lord of the Dead and the consort of the goddess Frigga. According to Norse mythology, Odin battled giants, seduced mortals and woke the dead in his quest for occult wisdom and absolute power. He is depicted as an old man with one eye, wearing a magickal ring and riding on an eight-legged horse. He is the equivalent of the Pagan-Germanic god Woden, and his sacred candle colors are purple, red and black.

OSIRIS

Ancient Egyptian god of vegetation and fertility, whose annual death and rebirth personified the self-renewing vitality and fertility of nature. He was also a ruler of the dead and both the brother and consort of the goddess Isis. According to Egyptian mythology, Osiris was drowned and torn into fourteen pieces by his jealous brother Set, but then restored to life through the magickal powers of Isis. His sacred candle colors are green and black.

PAN

Greek and Neo-Pagan horned-god of woodlands, fields, shepherds and fertility; often associated with the cult of Dionysus. He is depicted as a bearded man with the legs, horns and ears of a goat, and is the equivalent to the Roman nature deity Faunus. His sacred candle color is green.

PARVATI

Hindu goddess of mountains and consort of the god Shiva. She is known as the ruler of elves and nature spirits, the daughter of the Himalayas and the personification of cosmic energy. Her sacred candle colors are white and brown.

PELE

Polynesian Volcano-Goddess who is currently believed to reside in Kilauea on the main island of Mauna Loa, Hawaii, where she is worshipped as the essence of earthly fire. To this day, various offerings such as flowers, sugarcane, white birds, money and brandy are made to her whenever volcanic eruptions threaten the Hawaiian islands. Her sacred candle colors are red and orange.

PERSEPHONE
Greek goddess known as the Queen of the Underworld.
She is the equivalent of the Roman goddess Proserpina.
Her sacred candle color is black.

POMONA
Roman goddess of fruits and fertility. She is the consort
of the god Vertumnus (the Changer) and her festival of
Pomonalia was celebrated in ancient Rome on the first
day of November to mark the end of the harvest. Her
sacred candle color is green.

POSEIDON
Greek god of the sea, and one of the Twelve Great
Olympians whose Roman counterpart is Neptune. His
sacred candle color is light blue.

PTAH
God of ancient Egypt, who was believed to be the cre-
ator of the universe and the patron of architects, sculp-
tors and craftsmen. He was the consort of the lion-
headed goddess Sekhmet, and his cult was centered in
Memphis, Egypt where both he and his wife were worshipped. His sacred candle color is white.

QUETZALCOATL
Aztec god of fertility, wind and wisdom, personified as
a feather serpent and associated with the Morning Star.
His sacred candle colors are bronze and green. According to myth, Quetzalcoatl's twin brother was Xolotl, the
patron god of magicians. He personified the planet Venus as the Evening Star, and his sacred candle color is
black.

RA
Egyptian Sun-God; identified as a god of birth and rebirth. He was worshipped at Heliopolis and was the main deity in the Ennead. His sacred candle color is gold.

RHIANNON
Celtic/Welsh Mother-Goddess, originally called Rigatona (Great Queen) and identified with the Gaulish mare-goddess Epona as she is pictured riding astride a pale-white horse carrying a magickal bag of abundance. Her sacred candle color is white.

SATURN
Roman god of agriculture and harvest whose festival, the Saturnalia, was held annually in ancient Rome in mid-December. He is identified with the Greek god Cronus, and his sacred candle color is orange.

SEKHMET
War-Goddess of ancient Egypt and consort of the god Ptah. She is depicted as a woman with the head of a lion, and is the Egyptian counterpart of the Hindu goddess Shakti. Her sacred candle color is crimson.

SELENE
Greek Moon-Goddess in her waxing-moon aspect. In her waning-moon aspect, she is called Hecate. Her sacred candle colors are silver and white.

SET (also Seth)
Egyptian god of darkness and black magick and the personification of evil. He is the Egyptian counterpart of the Greek god Typhon. His sacred candle color is black.

SHAMASH
Babylonian Sun-God, brother of the goddess Ishtar and a deity associated with oracles of prophecy. He is identified with the Sumerian god Utu and the Greek god Apollo. His sacred candle color is yellow.

SIN
Babylonian god of the moon; identified with the Sumerian god Nanna. His sacred candle color is white.

SVAROG
Slavic god of fire and metalurgy, whose symbol is the silver hammer and tongs. He is the consort of the Great Mother and his sacred candle colors are red and silver.

SYLVANUS
Roman god of forests, fields and herding; depicted as a bearded satyr. His sacred candle color is dark green.

TANE
Polynesian Sky-God and lord of fertility, who is believed to have created the first man out of red clay. The tiki amulet (a human figure made of wood and mother-of-pearl) is a symbol of Tane's creative power. His sacred candle colors are blue and green.

THANATOS
Greek god of death whose Roman counterpart is the god Mors. His sacred candle color is black.

THOR
Scandinavian Sky-God, Master of Thunderbolts, son of Odin, and patron god of farmers and sailors. He is depicted as a strong but friendly man with wild hair and

a long, red beard. The hammer is his symbol and dark blue is his sacred candle color.

THOTH
Egyptian god of the moon, wisdom, magick, arts and science. He was also known as the scribe of the gods, and is depicted as an ibis, an ibis-headed man, and also as an ape. The truth-goddess Maat was his consort and the first month of the Egyptian year was named after him. His sacred candle colors are white, silver and purple.

THUNOR (also Donar)
Pagan-Germanic god of thunder and lightning and a deity associated with fertility. His sacred day of the week is Thursday, and dark blue, black and green are his sacred candle colors.

TIWAZ
Pagan-Germanic Sky-God and consort of the goddess Frija. His sacred candle color is blue.

TLAZOLTEOTL
Central American Earth-Goddess associated with fertility and love. She is also known as the "Mother of All Gods" and her sacred candle colors are brown and green.

TRIPLE GODDESS
A Goddess trinity having three different aspects and three different names. The Moon Mother is worshipped as a Triple Goddess whose sacred symbol is a crescent moon. Her three Goddess aspects correspond to the three lunar phases: In her waxing phase she is Selene the mother and giver of light. The full moon is Diana the huntress. In her waning phase she is Hecate the

wise crone and Queen of death and darkness. In Norse mythos, the trinity of the Triple Goddess is Freya (goddess of love and beauty), Frigga (mother-goddess) and Hel (queen of death and ruler of the underworld). The multiple aspects of the Celtic goddess Morrigan are: Macha, Badb and Neman. Even Mary of the Christian mythos is as much a trinity as any ancient Pagan goddess, although her followers do not describe her as such. She embodies the attributes found in the female deities of other cultures (Virgin, Mother, Saint) but suppressed by a paternal hierarchy, her worship as a Goddess is denied even by those who attend her rites. The sacred candle colors of the Triple Goddess are green (mother), red (warrior) and black (crone). There are also male God trinities such as the Hindu trimurti of Brahma, Vishnu and Shiva; the Greek sun-god triad of Apollo, Helios and Phoebus; and the well-known Christian union of three divine figures, the Father, Son and Holy Ghost, in one godhead. The sacred candle colors of the Triple God vary as the three aspects of the god are not always the same in each trinity.

URANUS (also Ouranos)
Ancient Greek god known as Father Sky. He was the consort of the goddess Gaea and personified the heavens. His sacred candle color is blue.

VENUS
Roman and Neo-Pagan goddess of love and beauty who personified sexuality, fertility, prosperity and good fortune. She is the Roman counterpart of the Greek Love-Goddess Aphrodite. Her sacred candle color is pink.

VESTA
Roman Hearth-Goddess whose temple was lit by a sacred fire tended by six virgin priestesses known as the Vestal Virgins. Her sacred candle color is red.

WODEN
Pagan-Germanic god of war, skald-craft (poetry), prophecy and magick, whose sacred day of the week is Wednesday. He was also known as the Lord of the Dead, the primeval runemaster, and the god of shape-shifting. Mythology shows Woden to be the highest deity of the German pantheon. The name "Woden" is the English form of the name ultimately derived from a Proto-Germanic form Wodh-an-az, meaning "the master of inspired psychic activity". As a Neo-Pagan god, he is worshipped mainly by Wiccans of the Saxon tradition, and is often identified with the Scandinavian god Odin, the mightiest of the Teutonic deities. His sacred candle colors are red and purple.

XOCHIQUETZAL
Central American goddess of flowers. Her sacred candle colors are white and all floral colors.

YARILO
Slavic Fertility-God and consort of the Moon-Goddess Marina. His sacred candle color is green.

ZEUS
The most powerful of the Greek gods, ruler of heaven and earth, and son of Kronos and Rhea. He was also known as the Cloud-Gatherer, the Lord of Thunderbolts and the master of shape-shifting. The oak was his sacred tree; the eagle his sacred bird, and gold his sacred candle color.

4

Candle Magick for Healing

Healing Herb Candles

The healing power of herbs should not be limited only
to brews and potions. Herbs should also be used in all
homemade candles crafted especially for healing spells
and rituals. (Store bought or non-herb candles can be
charged with healing herb power by being anointed
with an oil made from the appropriate herb.)

To make healing herb candles, place equal parts of
paraffin and beeswax in the top of a double boiler (or a
large metal can placed in a partially-filled pan of boiling
water) and melt over low heat.

Add a pinch of the appropriate healing herb(s) (powdered) to the melted wax and say:

O MAGICK HERBS OF ROOT AND FLOWER,
GIVE THIS CANDLE HEALING POWER.
LET ALL EVIL SICKNESS FLEE
WHEN IT IS BURNED, SO MOTE IT BE!

Cut waxed wicking to fit the size of the mold, allowing one extra inch of wick above the top of the mold. Attach a nut or screw to the bottom of each wick to serve as a weight, and then insert into the center of the mold.

Slowly pour the melted wax into the mold and allow it to cool and harden before removing the candle. (If a depression forms around the wick at the top of the candle after it has cooled, fill it with a little bit of melted wax and then let it cool. Repeat if necessary until the top of the candle is level.)

(IMPORTANT NOTE: Healing herb candles should always be crafted during the waxing of the moon to charge them with healing power, and burned during the moon's wane to decrease fevers, pains and ills.)

The following is a list of Witches' herbs and their magickal healing properties:

ADDER'S TONGUE: Stomach ulcers and tumors.
AGRIMONY: Jaundice and diseases of the liver.
ALDER: Diarrhea, inflammations and sore throat.
ALL-HEAL: External wounds.
ALOE VERA LEAVES: Burns and external wounds.
ANGELICA: Alcohol and drug abuse, delayed menstrual period, toothache pain.
ANISE: Bronchial asthma, bronchitis.
BLESSED THISTLE: Colds.

BLOODROOT: Ringworms.

CATNIP: Anxiety, fever, menstrual cramps.

CHAMOMILE: Colic, fever, inflammations, menstrual cramps and nervous conditions.

CHICKWEED: Inflammations.

CINNAMON: Flu.

COLTSFOOT: Bronchial asthma, bronchitis, chest complaints and coughs.

COMFREY: Dysentery, external wounds and stomach ulcers.

CORIANDER: Fever.

COSTMARY: Infections.

CRIMSON CLOVER: Cancers.

DAISY: Bronchial asthma.

DANDELION: Constipation, gall stones and ailments of the liver, pancreas, spleen or female organs.

DOGWOOD: Fevers and infections.

ELDERFLOWERS: Colds, constipation, fever, hemorrhoids and impotency.

ELECAMPANE: Coughs and irregular menstruation.

EYEBRIGHT: Eye ailments.

FENNEL: Anxiety, constipation and irregular menstrual periods.

GARLIC: Arthritis, bronchial asthma, infections and rheumatism.

GINGER: Fever, impotency and menstrual cramps.

GINSENG: Impotency and all sexually-related ailments.

GOLDENROD: Bladder infections, inflammations and insomnia.

GOLDENSEAL: Eczema, eye ailments, internal infections, poison ivy, rectal ulcers and ringworms.

HAWTHORN: Arteriosclerosis, edema, heart ailments and weak muscles.

HOREHOUND: Colds, coughs and constipation.

HORSEHEAL: Fever.

HORSERADISH ROOT: Bronchitis, colds, kidney conditions and rheumatism.

IRISH MOSS: Burns and coughs.

JACOB'S LADDER: Fever.

JASMINE: Impotency.

JIMSONWEED: Poison ivy.

JUNIPER: Neuralgic pains, rheumatism and swellings.

LADY'S MANTLE: Fever, headaches, inflammations, insomnia, menopause, menstrual cramps and toothache.

LAVENDER: Depression, fatigue, headache, impotency, neuralgic pains, rheumatism and sprains.

LIFEROOT: Menopause and menstrual problems.

MALLOW: Tonsilitis.

MANDRAKE ROOT: Impotency and infertility.

MILKWEED: Warts.

MOTHERWORT: All female problems.

MUGWORT: Fever and poison ivy.

MULLEIN LEAVES: Bronchial asthma.

MYRRH: Gum irritations and pain.

NETTLE: Bronchial asthma, muscle aches, stomach ulcers, and diseases of the lungs and intestines.

PASSIONFLOWER:: Insomnia.

PENNYROYAL: Fever and menstrual cramps.

PEPPERMINT: Headaches and muscle cramps.

ROSE: Kidney stones.

ROSEMARY: Colds, colic, congestion of the liver, depression, fatigue, headaches, high blood pressure, nervous heart conditions, paralysis, rheumatism, stress, weakness of the limbs and vertigo.

SAFFRON: Depression and fever.

SAGE: Colds and coughs, depression, fever, flu, insomnia, pleurisy, sprains and varicose veins.

SCABWORT ROOT: Fever and infections.

SERPENTERIA ROOT: Impotency and snakebite.

SHEPHERD'S PURSE: Bruises, skin irritations and rheumatism.

SOLOMON'S SEAL:: Bruises, skin irritations and wounds.

ST. JOHN'S WORT: Diarrhea.

STRAWBERRY LEAVES AND FLOWERS: Gout.

THYME: Fever, headaches and whooping cough.

VALERIAN: Anxiety, insomnia, rheumatism, stress and swollen joints.

VERVAIN: Fever.

VIOLET: Infections.

WILLOW BARK: Headaches.

WITCH HAZEL: Anxiety, eczema, inflammations, swellings and tumors.

WORMWOOD: Colds and fever.

YARROW: Canker sores, colds, fever, liver diseases and muscle aches.

Lunar Healing Ritual

Each of the 12 signs of the zodiac rules different areas of the anatomy.

The parts of the body ruled by an individual sign may either be the strongest (healthiest) or weakest physical areas of a person born under that particular astrological sign. They may also be a combination of the two. For instance, the sign of Capricorn rules the knees, bones, teeth and skin; therefore, a Capricornian may find that he or she was born with strong, healthy bones and teeth, but prone to have skin problems. On the other hand, the Capricornian may have a perfect "peaches and cream" complexion and suffer from orthopaedic and dental troubles, or perhaps rheumatism.

When healing a specific area of the body, it is vital that the healing candle ritual be performed during the proper lunar time when the moon is in the astrological sign which influences that particular part of the body.

A *white* candle should always be used in healing rituals as white is the color that symbolizes healing energy, purification and the power of the sacred Goddess.

The ritual may be performed at any hour of the day or night (the time is unimportant) as long as the moon is in the correct sign. (The moon changes from one sign in the zodiac to the next approximately every two and one-half days. It is best to consult an up to date astrological or lunar calendar to find out the exact days and times each moon sign begins and ends.)

> *MOON IN ARIES*: influences the head and brain.
> *MOON IN TAURUS*: influences the throat and neck.

MOON IN GEMINI: influences shoulders, arms and lungs.

MOON IN CANCER: influences the chest and stomach.

MOON IN LEO: influences the upper back, spine and heart.

MOON IN VIRGO: influences the intestines and nervous system.

MOON IN LIBRA: influences the lower back and kidneys.

MOON IN SCORPIO: influences the reproductive organs.

MOON IN SAGITTARIUS: influences the liver, thighs and hips.

MOON IN CAPRICORN: influences knees, bones, teeth and skin.

MOON IN AQUARIUS: influences calves, ankles and blood.

MOON IN PISCES: influences the feet and lymph glands.

Cast a healing circle on the ground about nine feet in diameter using white chalk or paint. (A circle of small white stones could also be cast if the ritual is to take place outdoors.)

Sprinkle a bit of salt over the center of the circle and then at the east, south, west and north ends. As you do this, say:

WITH THIS SACRED SALT
I CONSECRATE THIS CIRCLE.
LET ALL EVIL SPIRITS
BE CAST FORTH HENCEFROM!
LET ALL NEGATIVE VIBRATIONS
BE CAST FORTH HENCEFROM!

LET ALL IMPURITIES AND HINDRANCES
BE CAST FORTH HENCEFROM!
AND LET ALL THAT IS POSITIVE AND GOOD
ENTER HEREIN.
BLESSED BE THIS HEALING CIRCLE
IN THE NAME OF THE GODDESS.
SO MOTE IT BE.

Erect a small alter in the center of the circle facing north. Arrange on top of it the following consecrated tools necessary for this healing ritual: white candle and athame in the center, censer of incense to the east as a symbol of the element Air, ceremonial sword to the south as a symbol of the element Fire, chalice of white wine (or water) to the west as a symbol of the element Water, and pentacle (a round disk of wax or metal inscribed with the five-pointed Witches' star) to the north as a symbol of the element Earth. In front of the candle, place a photograph of the person in need of healing.

With the ceremonial sword in your right hand, trace the circle, starting at the east and moving in a clockwise direction. As you trace the circle, say:

I CONJURE THEE
O SACRED CIRCLE OF WHITE
THAT THOU BEIST A DIVINE
CIRCLE OF HEALING POWER.
ONCE AGAIN DO I BLESS THEE
AND CONSECRATE THEE
IN THE NAME OF THE GODDESS.
SO MOTE IT BE.

Return the sword to the altar. Light the candle and incense. Take the athame in your right hand and gently pass the blade through the rising smoke of the incense three times and say:

> YOD HE VAU HE
> I INVOKE THEE
> ELEMENTAL KING OF THE EAST.

Tap the blade of the ceremonial sword three times with the tip of the athame and say:

> ADONAI
> I INVOKE THEE
> ELEMENTAL KING OF THE SOUTH.

Dip the blade of the athame into the chalice of wine and say:

> EHEIEH
> I INVOKE THEE
> ELEMENTAL KING OF THE SOUTH.

Trace the pentacle with the tip of the athame and say:

> AGLA
> I INVOKE THEE
> ELEMENTAL KING OF THE NORTH.

Take the athame now in both hands and point it up to the heavens with both arms outstretched and say:

> GODDESS OF LIFE
> GODDESS OF LOVE
> SEND YOUR HEALING POWER FROM ABOVE

INTO THIS CIRCLE CONSECRATED TO THEE
SO THAT (name of person) MAY BE HEALED
SO MOTE IT BE.

Close your eyes and visualize a radiating beam of white light coming down from the sky into the tip of the athame and then down into your arms and body, filling your insides with a warm, glowing, tingling feeling. Continue visualizing and when you start to feel the divine healing power of the Goddess building up within you, begin a visualization of the person in need of healing. Concentrate hard and see that person in your mind's eye completely cured of their ailment and in perfect health.

Point the athame at the photograph (or at the actual person if he or she participates in the ritual). Direct and then release the built-up healing energy into the ailing person. Allow the energy to again build up within you and then direct and release it. Continue until all of the energy has been used up.

Relax for a few minutes (this ritual can be physically exhausting) and then give thanks to the Goddess for her presence and help.

With the ceremonial sword in your left hand, trace the circle in a counter-clockwise direction starting in the east to uncast the circle.

Let the candle burn itself out.

used by many healers as a blood purifier, and it is reputed to be effective in the treatment of acne, asthma, bronchitis, depression, excema, goiter, hair loss, hay fever, lung ailments, malaria, psoriasis, throat irritations, ulcers and urinary tract infections.

AMETHYST is a stone of power, peace, protection and spirituality. It balances the aura, eases tension and brings contentment and sincerity into the lives of those who use it. Amethyst aids spiritual and psychic development, and can be used as a powerful meditation stone. As a healing gemstone, amethyst is reputed to be effective in the treatment of such ailments as allergies, blood clots, brain tumors, diabetes, dropsy, eating disorders, glaucoma, hallucinations, headaches, insomnia, Parkinson's disease, sinusitis, stress, urinary problems and venereal diseases.

AQUAMARINE symbolizes hope and confidence. Its name is Latin for "seawater" and when worn as an amulet, it offers protection for sailors and other travelers of the sea. Aquamarine enhances meditation and spiritual awareness, and as a healing gemstone, it is reputed to be effective in the treatment of such ailments as anxiety, coughs, ear aches, headaches, insomnia, laryngitis, liver disorders, swollen glands, toothaches, upset stomach and vascular diseases. (For best results, it is recommended that aquamarine be wrapped in copper wire and placed in direct sunlight for several hours to absorb solar prana energy before being used as a healing stone.)

BERYL is known as both the "Mystic Stone" and the "Seer's Stone." Yellow or golden beryl increases psychic abilities when placed on the area of the forehead known as the third eye, or when held in the left hand during meditation rituals. Beryl has long been used by seers as a scrying stone and as a dowsing stone to locate hidden or lost things. It possesses the power to banish fear and sharpen the mind. When worn as a magickal charm, it attracts the affections of the opposite sex. As a healing gemstone, beryl is reputed to be effective in the treatment of constipation, depression, diarrhea, exhaustion, nausea, obesity and ulcers.

BLOODSTONE, a variety of chalcedony, is also called heliotrope. In the Middle Ages, magicians and sorcerers believed that the state of invisibility could be acquired by combining the stone heliotrope with the mystical flower of the same name. Bloodstone sends out healing vibrations and brings harmony into the lives of those who wear it or carry it in a mojo bag. Bloodstone is very cold to the touch and is often used to slow blood flow from a wound (hence its name). As a healing gemstone, bloodstone is reputed to be effective in the treatment of anemia, fevers, hemorrhoids, inflammations, insect bites and menstrual problems. Bloodstone is also known to be a mental stimulant and a blood purifier.

CARNELIAN is a legendary stone of good luck. In ancient times, people in Egypt wore amulets made of carnelian to protect themselves from the wrath of the mighty Sun God and to counteract the power of the Evil Eye. Carnelian as a fertility stone purifies the blood and hormones, stimulates feelings of sexual arousal, and aids sexual function, orgasm and conception. As a healing gemstone, carnelian is reputed to be effective in the treatment of such ailments as arthritis, asthma, colds, constipation, depression, epilepsy, exhaustion, infections, lung diseases, menstrual cramps, mental disorders, poor blood circulation and sinus pain. Carnelian can also be worn in a mojo bag between the breasts to increase breast milk in nursing women.

CORAL, one of the most magickal of gemstones, is actually not a stone at all, but a hard, rock-like structure created by the calcium deposits of tiny sea polyp organisms. It is said that coral could be used to detect poisons in food and drink, cure bleeding, and protect its wearer against being struck by bolts of lightning as well as other misfortunes. It was common for children in ancient Rome to wear a piece of coral on a necklace for protection against sorcerers and devils. In other parts of the world, it was worn as a charm to increase wisdom and keep away ghosts. However, coral is probably best known for its use in Italy as a powerful countercharm against the dreaded *mal d'occhio* (evil eye). Coral is a sacred stone to the tribal people of Polynesia and the Hawaiian islands, and in Pueblo Indian symbolism, it is one of the four elemental gemstones. In the 17th Century, coral was crushed to a powder, mixed with wine or water and ingested to purify the blood, increase beauty and cure fluxes of the belly, malfunctions of the womb, fits, convulsions, emaciations and rickets. Powdered coral was also used in ancient spells against tempests and the perils of flood. As a healing gemstone, coral stimulates sexual energy, aids fertility and removes impurities from the blood and aura. It is also reputed to be effective in the treatment of such ailments as allergies, arthritis, asthma, bladder infections, calcium deficiencies, congestion, coughs, depression, indigestion, lung problems and muscle weakness.

DIAMOND is the symbol of fidelity, innocence, peace and serenity. When worn as a magickal charm, it prevents nightmares and brings confidence, divine wisdom and consciousness. It is said that when held in the left hand, a diamond will ward off wild and venomous beasts, enemies, and even madness. Diamonds are the most powerful of all gemstones for balancing both positive and negative energies, and are reputed to be effective in treating acne problems, gout, heart conditions and insomnia. (It is important that diamonds be cleared of negativity before using as a healing stone. This can be done by simply burying the diamond in the earth or in a container of dry sea salt for 24 hours.)

EMERALD, the symbol of love and peace, is a mystical gemstone dedicated to the South American love goddess Esmeralda. In the Middle Ages, emeralds were believed to be found in the nests of mythological half-eagle, half-lion beasts called griffins. When worn or carried as an amulet, an emerald strengthens love, intelligence, eloquence and popularity, and it was believed that emerald charms worn by pregnant women offered them protection against miscarriages. Another ancient belief was that an emerald placed under the tongue could give a mortal man the power to prophesy. Emerald increases psychic sensitivity and as a healing gemstone, it is reputed to be effective in the treatment of depression, epilepsy, fever and pancreatic disorders.

FLUORITE increases psychic awareness and cosmic understanding when placed on the third eye area of the forehead during meditative rituals. As a healing gemstone, fluorite is reputed to be effective in the treatment of such ailments as insomnia, mental disorders, nervous conditions, Parkinson's disease, stress and tumors of the brain.

GARNET, also known as the "Passion Stone," is a balancer of the yin and yang energies. It increases psychic sensitivity and sexual energy. Garnet is an ideal gemstone to use during meditative rituals, and can be worn as a charm to attract sexual love and soul mates. When placed under a pillow or worn while sleeping, it wards off evil dreams. As a healing gemstone, garnet is reputed to be effective in the treatment of such ailments as anemia, depression, frostbite, impotency, menstrual cramps, neuralgia and paralysis.

HEMATITE was used by ancient Roman and Greek warriors as a charm for protection against wounds and to increase courage. It is reputed to be effective in the treatment of such ailments as bladder and kidney problems, bloodshot eyes, high blood pressure, insomnia and wounds.

JACINTH, also known as hyacinth, aids astral projection and increases psychic powers. It is often worn or carried as an amulet for the attainment of honor, prudence and wisdom, as well as for protection against poisoning, lightning, injuries and wounds. As a healing gemstone, jacinth is reputed to be effective in the treatment of insomnia, lung diseases, polio and tuberculosis.

JADE symbolizes peace, tranquility and wisdom. It is also the symbol of immortality and a sacred stone to the ancient Chinese goddess of healing mercy. It is said that immortality can be achieved by powdering and eating a green jade. When worn as a magickal charm, it brings long life and prevents nightmares. Jade has long been used in the magickal ceremonies and rituals of many different cultures including the ancient Mayans who used sacred knives with blades of jade in their infamous human sacrifices. Black jade is used in Chinese magick, particularly in necromantic practices. As a healing gemstone, jade is reputed to be effective in the treatment of such ailments as anxiety, disorders of the bladder and kidneys, emotional pain, fear, indigestion, stress and urinary problems.

JASPER is an energizing gemstone that strengthens the intellect when worn as an amulet with certain cabalistic inscriptions. As a healing gemstone, jasper is reputed to be effective for purifying the blood and treating bladder infections, epilepsy, menstrual cramps and nausea.

JET, also known as both the "Exorcism Stone" and the "Stone of Mourning," is best known for its long-time use in women's mourning jewelry. When powdered and burned, it emits powerful fumes that are used to exorcize demonic spirits and unpleasant apparitions. In Iceland, jet is carried as an amulet for protection against devils. In Africa, it is placed under the threshold of an enemy to curse him. Jet was also used in Medieval Europe to test virginity. As a healing gemstone, it is reputed to be effective in the treatment of such ailments as dropsy, epilepsy, fever, hallucinations, headaches, hysteria, lymphatic swelling, stomach diseases and toothache.

LAPIS LAZULI is a powerful love-drawing gemstone dedicated to the goddesses Aphrodite, Venus and Isis. It aids meditation and psychic development, and has frequently been used by Witches in love spells. As a healing stone, lapis lazuli is reputed to be effective in the treatment of such ailments as bleeding, burns, degenerative nerve diseases, depression, epilepsy, eye ailments, fever, headaches, heart diseases, high blood pressure, infections, inflammations, insomnia, menopause, menstrual cramps, mental disorders, migraines, multiple sclerosis, sore throat pain, stress, surgical recovery and swellings.

LODESTONES, natural magnets, have long been used by practitioners of magick to set up energy fields that block out negative vibrations. In days of old, lodestone amulets were worn to protect one from snakebites, and it is said that a lodestone placed in the right ear will enable a mortal to hear the voices of the gods.

Lodestones are reputed to be effective in the treatment of headaches, hearing defects, minor flesh wounds and weak eyes.

MALACHITE, the symbol of creativity and change, is the oldest of all healing gemstones. It possesses a balancing vibration that restores tired nerves, increases vitality, absorbs negativity and purifies the blood and aura. The ancient Egyptians used crushed malachite as a powerful eyeshadow to ward off the evil eye. They also believed that malachite increased the psychic powers and gave man the power to communicate with the dead. As a healing gemstone, it is reputed to be effective in the treatment of bladder infections, colic, diseases of the liver, dyslexia, irregular menstruation, muscle spasms, nervous disorders and paranoia. Malachite should be frequently cleansed of all negative energies which it absorbs into itself, otherwise it will grow dull and lose its healing power. The best way to clear malachite of absorbed negativity is to place it on a clear quartz crystal cluster for three or more hours and then anoint it with oil of Frankincense and Myrrh.

MOONSTONE, also known as both the "Hope Stone" and the "Dream Stone," symbolizes chastity and purity, and is sacred to the lunar Triple Goddess: Diana, Selene, Hecate. As a stone of magick, moonstone is used in astral projections, Goddess invocations, moon rituals, meditative rituals, healing spells and wish magick. It increases psychic power and sensitivity and is a balancer of feminine energy. As a luck-attracting charm, it is most powerful when worn by persons born under the Moon-ruled sign of Cancer. Moonstone is regarded as a sacred fertility stone in Arabia where it is hung on the branches of fruit trees in blossom for plentiful fruit. It is said that a moonstone in a rainwater bath will make fertile a woman unable to bear children. As a healing gemstone, moonstone is reputed to be effective in treating cancers, colds, flu, infertility, insomnia, irregular menstruation, menopause and premenstrual syndrome.

ONYX is a mystical stone that absorbs and transforms negative energy without storing it as do many other gemstones. Once thought to be an unlucky stone, it was regarded as the symbol of death, sorrow and fear. An onyx amulet protects its wearer from danger and misfortunes, stimulates the mind, brings courage and strength, increases spiritual wisdom, and dispels negativity. Onyx is often used for magickal jewelry, sacred statues, altar tools, pyramids and fetishes. It is ruled by the planet Saturn and therefore possesses a powerful Capricorn/Aquarius vibration. As a healing gemstone, onyx is reputed to be effective in the treatment of bone weaknesses, emotional suffering, heart diseases, ulcers, and problems of the skin, teeth, hair and fingernails.

OPAL was considered a stone of purity and good fortune in the Orient and also in ancient Rome and Greece where it was valued highly for prophecy. However, in Europe, opal is believed to be the bringer of bad luck, misery and death. In the United States as well, opals are regarded as unlucky stones except when worn as birth-charms by persons born under the sign of Libra. In the 13th Century, opal was believed to be a magickal stone with the power to make a man invisible when wrapped in the leaf of a laurel or bay tree and held in the hand. In Italy during the great plague of the Middle Ages, it was said that an opal worn by a person who had caught the dread disease glowed bright and then faded after the wearer died. In the 19th Century, an unlucky (or perhaps cursed) opal ring supposedly caused the deaths of Alphonso XII of Spain, his wife, sister and sister-in-law. As a powerful Libran amulet, opal increases clairvoyant powers, balances the psyche, sharpens the memory, attracts good fortune and gives healing power to the wearer.

RUBY, the stone of courage and loyalty, possesses intense energy and is a stimulator of sexuality, physical vitality, mental concentration and emotional energy. As a powerful amulet, ruby works best for those born under the sign of Leo. It brings peace of mind and prevents all evil and impure thoughts. In the Middle Ages, rubies were worn by priests who believed the stone to be a strong protector of chastity. As a healing gemstone, ruby is reputed to be effective in the treatment of anemia, blood poisoning, cancer, depression, exhaustion, fatigue, infertility, leukemia, snakebite, sterility, and ailments of the heart, kidneys and liver.

SAPPHIRE symbolizes harmony and peace and is an excellent gemstone to use in love spells and meditation rituals. When worn as an amulet, it brings happiness and contentment and protects its wearer against misfortune, violence, psychic attack and accidental death. As a healing gemstone, sapphire is reputed to be effective in the treatment of Alzheimer's disease, burns, degenerative nerve disease, fevers, hemorrhoids, infections, inflammations, insomnia, multiple sclerosis, nosebleeds, sore throat and ulcers.

TOPAZ is an energizing gemstone which stimulates the intellect and dispels negativity. Topaz can be used as a divining rod to locate buried treasures or underground water, and when worn as an amulet, it protects its wearer against injury or attack. As a healing gemstone, topaz is reputed to be effective in the treatment of such ailments as depression, diseases of the bone, insomnia, sexual dysfunctions, shock and stress.

TOURMALINE is the symbol of vitality. As a magickal gemstone, it can be carried in a mojo bag as a charm to protect against illness, used as a psychic healing wand or worn as magickal jewelry to attract a lover. *Black Tourmaline* deflects negativity, dispels fears and re-balances the aura. It connects the physical with the spiritual and reduces anger, jealousy and feelings of insecurity. It is also an ideal stone to use in meditation rituals. Black tourmaline is reputed to be effective in treating such ailments as anxiety, constipation, depression, diarrhea, stress and ulcers. *Green Tourmaline*, also known as verdelite, possesses the power to attract money and success. As a healing gemstone, it is reputed to be effective in the treatment of constipation, fatigue, fever, flu, gall stones, high blood pressure, indigestion, infections, inflammations, muscle aches, swellings and toothache. *Pink Tourmaline*, also known as rubellite, calms, reduces fear, protects the aura against negativity and induces peaceful sleep. *Watermelon Tourmaline* heals the emotions, balances sexual energies and stabilizes the yin/yang polarities. As a healing gemstone, it is reputed to be effective in the treatment of cancer and degenerative nerve diseases. *Yellow Tourmaline* stimulates the brain, strengthens the psychic powers and increases wisdom and understanding.

TURQUOISE is a mystical gemstone sacred to the Native Americans of the southwest United States. It is one of the four elemental stones in Pueblo Indian symbolism, and is called the "Sky Stone" by the Navahos. Turquoise is the traditional wedding stone in Russia. In Arabia, it is used as a meditation stone, and in the Orient, it is used as a protective charm for horses and their riders. Turquoise should be carried on Wednesdays to attract good luck and protect against evil influences. A carved piece of turquoise brings good fortune

into a house and is said to possess the power to hypno-
tize wild animals. Turquoise is often worn as an evil eye
countercharm, used in spells of love and desire, and
carried or worn as a charm to protect against venomous
bites, blindness, assassinations and accidental deaths.
Turquoise absorbs negative feelings and possesses a
strong healing vibration. Turquoise changes colors to
warn its wearer of impending bad health and is reputed
to be effective in the treatment of such ailments as
asthma, burns, diseases of the lungs, fevers, high blood
pressure, inflammations, migraines, swellings, tension
and trauma.

5

Sabbat Candle Rituals

The Four Grand Witches' Sabbats

February 2nd: CANDLEMAS (Imbolc, Oimelc)
May 1st: BELTANE (Walpurgisnacht, May Day)
August 1st: LAMMAS (Lughnasadh)
October 31st: SAMHAIN (Halloween)

The Four Lesser Sabbats*

VERNAL EQUINOX (Spring Sabbat/Rite of Eostre)
SUMMER SOLSTICE (Midsummer Sabbat)
AUTUMN EQUINOX SABBAT
WINTER SOLSTICE (Yule Sabbat)

*Each year the astronomical dates of the four lesser Sabbats change. To find out the exact date of each festival, consult an up-to-date astrological calendar or any other current calendar of days showing the exact dates of the equinoxes and solstices.

Candlemas: The Feast of Lights

FEBRUARY 2nd

The Candlemas Sabbat, also known as Imbolc, Oimelc, and Lady Day, is a fire festival celebrating the Goddess of Fertility and her consort, the Great Horned God. In ancient times, it was celebrated as the Feast of Pan.

Erect an altar, facing north. Place before it a consecrated besom (a straw broom). Prepare a crown of 13 red candles and place it on the center of the altar. At each side of the crown, place a brown or pink candle. To the left, place a censer of wisteria incense and a sprig of evergreen. (A sprig from a Yule tree or wreath may be used.) To the right, place a chalice of water, a small dish of dirt or sand and an athame.

Cast a circle around the altar using white chalk or paint. Sprinkle a bit of salt inside the circle and then trace the circle in a clockwise direction with a ceremonial sword and say:

WITH SALT AND SACRED SWORD
I CONSECRATE AND INVOKE THEE
O SABBAT CIRCLE OF MAGICK AND LIGHT.

BLESSED BE IN THE DIVINE NAME
OF THE FERTILITY GODDESS
AND HER CONSORT, THE GREAT HORNED ONE.

Place the ceremonial sword on the altar before the crown of candles. Light the two altar candles and say:

> O GODDESS AND GOD
> I OFFER TO THEE
> THIS SYMBOL OF FIRE
> SO MOTE IT BE.

Light the incense and say:

> O GODDESS AND GOD
> I OFFER TO THEE
> THIS SYMBOL OF AIR
> SO MOTE IT BE.

Take the athame in your right hand and with the tip of the blade, draw a pentacle (five-pointed star) in the dirt or sand and say:

> O GODDESS AND GOD
> I OFFER TO THEE
> THIS SYMBOL OF EARTH
> SO MOTE IT BE.

Dip the blade of the athame into the chalice of water and say:

> O GODDESS AND GOD
> I OFFER TO THEE
> THIS SYMBOL OF WATER
> SO MOTE IT BE.

Return the athame to the altar. Light the evergreen sprig and visualize in your mind's eye the darkness of winter burning away, being replaced by the warm light of spring. Place the burning sprig in the censer and say:

> AS THIS SYMBOL OF WINTER
> IS CONSUMED BY THE FIRE
> SO IS THE DARKNESS
> CONSUMED BY THE LIGHT.
> SO MOTE IT BE.

Light the crown of candles and carefully place it on top of your head. (When the rite is performed by a Coven, it is customary for the High Priest to light the candles and place the crown upon the head of the High Priestess.) Take the athame in your right hand and hold it over your heart as you say:

> LIKE SWEET CYBELE, I WEAR A CROWN
> OF FIRE AROUND MY HEAD.
> LIKE DIANA, BLESSED GODDESS WISE
> I LIGHT THE CANDLES RED
> TO SHINE A LIGHT UPON MY PRAYER
> FOR PEACE ON EARTH AND LOVE.
> O HEAR ME SPIRITS OF THE AIR,
> SPIRITS BELOW AND SPIRITS ABOVE.
> SO MOTE IT BE!

Return the athame to the altar and end the rite by sweeping the circle in a counter-clockwise direction with the besom to uncast the circle and to symbolize the "sweeping out" of the old.

Beltane

The Beltane festival is derived from an ancient Druid fire festival celebrating the union of the Goddess and the Horned God, and thus is also a fertility festival. (In the Old Religion, "fertility" signified the desire to produce more from the farms and fields, not erotic activity per se.)

Beltane marks the "death" of winter and the "birth" of spring, and is one of the Pagan festivals that have survived from pre-Christian times to modern day in much of its original form.

The festival of Beltane, also known as May Day, May Eve, and Walpurgisnacht, is based in part on Floralia, an old Roman nature festival dedicated to Flora, the sacred Flower Goddess. The first day of May was also the day when the ancient Romans burned frankincense and Solomon's Seal and hung wildflower wreaths before their altars in honor of the guardian spirits who watched over their families and homes.

Beltane begins with the lighting of bonfires at midnight on the last day of April. A Sabbat ritual in honor of the Goddess is performed, followed by a celebration of nature which consists of feasts and games and the singing of sacred songs. The mirth and merriment continues on into the wee morning hours and at dawn on May Day, morning dew is gathered from grass and wildflowers to be used in mystical potions for good luck.

Beltane Sabbat Ritual

The following Sabbat ritual is traditionally performed at midnight high on a hilltop where the huge Beltane bonfires are lit to light the way for summer.

In addition to the bonfire, Beltane rushlights are also lit and placed around the circle which is decorated with flowers and candles.

To make Beltane rushlights, strip off the skin from mature cattails (rushes) and dip the pith in melted wax or tallow in the same way that Voodoo candles are dipped. (See page 168) After the dipped rushlights have cooled and hardened, they are ready to be lit and enjoyed. (IMPORTANT NOTE: Beltane rushlights are intended for use only in *outdoor* rituals as the flames have a tendency to be quite erratic.)

If the Sabbat is celebrated indoors, a Beltane fire may be burned in a fireplace, or 13 dark green candles may be lit instead if you do not have a fireplace.

Dress in bright springtime colors (unless you prefer to work skyclad) and wear lots of colorful and fragrant flowers in your hair. (Before dressing for the ceremony, you should meditate and bathe by candlelight in an herbal bath to cleanse the body and soul of impurities.)

Cast a large circle and erect an altar in the middle of it, facing east. On top of the altar, in the center, place a small statue to represent the Goddess, and on each side of the statue, place a white altar candle. On the left side of the altar, place a censer containing frankincense and Solomon's Seal. On the right side of the altar, place an athame and a chalice filled with wine. Light 13 dark green candles and place them around the circle.

Prepare a crown of springtime wildflowers such as daisies, primroses, yellow cowslips or marigolds, and place the crown on the altar before the symbol of the Goddess.

A small Maypole about three feet in height may be erected at the right of the altar and decorated with flowers and bright colored ribbons.

Kneel before the altar. Light the altar candles and incense. Close your eyes, concentrate on the image of the Goddess, and say:

O GODDESS OF ALL THINGS WILD AND FREE
THIS PLACE I CONSECRATE TO THEE

Return to your feet. Take your athame from the altar, hold it out in salute toward the east and say:

BLESSED BE THE MAID OF SPRING
TO HER THIS PRAYER OF LOVE I SING

Hold your athame out in salute toward the south and say:

SHE MAKES THE WOODS AND MEADOWS
    GREEN
O GODDESS OF NATURE
SHE REIGNS SUPREME

Hold your athame out in salute toward the west and say:

FRANKINCENSE AND SOLOMON'S SEAL
HAIL TO SHE WHO TURNS THE WHEEL

Hold your athame out in salute toward the north and say:

SACRED BELTANE FIRE BURN
THE GODDESS OF FERTILITY HAS RETURNED

Return the athame to the top of the altar. Take the crown of wildflowers and place it on top of your head. Kneel before the altar, facing the image of the Goddess. Hold your arms out and say:

SPIRITS OF THE WATER AND AIR
I ASK THEE NOW TO HEAR MY PRAYER
LET THE SKY AND SEA BE CLEAN
LET THE LAND BE FERTILE GREEN.
SPIRITS OF THE FIRE
SPIRITS OF THE MOTHER EARTH
LET THE WORLD BE BLESSED
WITH PEACE, LOVE AND MIRTH.

Raise up the chalice of wine. Hold it out at arm's length and, as you pour a tiny bit of wine on the ground as a libation to the Goddess, close your eyes and say:

SACRED BELTANE FIRES BURN
LIGHT THE WAY FOR SUN'S RETURN
WINTER'S DARKNESS NOW MUST END
THE GREAT WHEEL OF LIFE HAS TURNED
    AGAIN.

Drink the rest of the wine from the chalice and return it to the altar. Put out the candles and incense.

The ritual is now complete and should be followed by a joyous celebration of feasting, singing and dancing.

Lammas

AUGUST 1st

Lammas (also known as Lughnasadh and August Eve) is the first Festival of Harvest.

It was originally celebrated by the ancient Druids as Lughnasadh to pay homage to Lugh, the Celtic sun god. In other pre-Christian Pagan cultures, Lammas was celebrated as a festival of bread and as a day to honor the death of the Sacred King.

On Lammas, homemade breads and berry pies are traditionally baked and eaten in honor of the harvest.

The making of corn dollies (small figures fashioned from braided straw) is another old Lammas custom. The corn dollies (or kirn babies, as they are sometimes called) are placed on the Sabbat altar to symbolize the Mother Goddess of the harvest. It is customary on Lammas to make (or buy) a new corn dolly and then burn the old one from the past year for good luck.

Lammas Sabbat Ritual

Cast a circle about nine feet in diameter. Erect an an altar in the center of the circle, facing north. On the altar, place a yellow candle. To the left of the candle (west), place a metal tray or dish containing a new corn dolly and the one from last year's Sabbat. To the right of the candle (east), place a censer of sandalwood or rose incense, and a cup or bowl containing Lammas Ritual Potpourri. (See recipe immediately following this Sabbat ritual.) Before the candle (south), place a consecrated athame and a ceremonial sword.

Sprinkle a bit of salt to consecrate the circle and then, starting in the east, trace the circle with the tip of the ceremonial sword, moving in a clockwise direction, and say:

> IN THE SACRED NAME OF THE GODDESS
> AND UNDER HER PROTECTION
> IS THIS SABBAT RITE NOW BEGUN.

Light the incense and candle and say:

> O GODDESS, BRIGHTER THAN THE STARS
> LET THY DIVINE LIGHT SHINE FORTH
> TO ILLUMINATE THE DARKNESS.
> SO MOTE IT BE.

Take the new corn dolly and place it to the right of the candle and say:

> O LADY OF THE HARVEST
> I GIVE THEE THANKS
> FOR SUSTAINING US IN SEASONS TO COME

BY THE BOUNTY OF THIS HARVEST.
SO MOTE IT BE.

Take the old corn dolly and light it with the flame of the candle. Place it on the metal tray or dish and as it burns, say:

LADY OF HARVEST PAST, NOW BURN
TO THE GODDESS YE SHALL RETURN
BLESS ME WITH THE LUCK AND LOVE
OF GOD AND GODDESS UP ABOVE.
SO MOTE IT BE!

End the rite by putting out the candle and uncasting the circle in a counter-clockwise direction with the ceremonial sword. Bury the ashes of the old corn dolly in the earth and save the new corn dolly for next Lammas.

LAMMAS RITUAL POTPOURRI

20 drops clove bud oil
25 drops sandalwood oil
1 cup oak moss
2 cups dried pink rose buds
2 cups dried red peony petals
1 cup dried amaranth flowers
1 cup dried heather flowers
½ cup dried cornflowers

Mix the clove bud and sandalwood oils with the oak moss and then add the rest of the ingredients. Stir well and then store in a tightly covered ceramic or glass container.

Place in a cup or bowl on the altar at Lammas as a fragrant ritual potpourri or cast it into an open fire or sprinkle it on hot charcoal blocks and burn as a powerful ritual incense. (Lammas Potpourri may also be put into a mojo bag and carried or worn to attract a lover.)

Samhain

OCTOBER 31st

Samhain (also known as Halloween and Hallows Eve) is celebrated on the last day of October through November 1st, and is the ancient Celtic/Druid New Year, the beginning of the cider season, and the most important of all the Witches' Sabbats.

Samhain celebrates the end of the Goddess-ruled summer and marks the arrival of the God-ruled winter. (The name Samhain means "Summer's End.")

It is the time when spirits of deceased loved ones and friends are honored, and at one time in history, many believed that it was the night when the dead returned to walk among the living.

In many parts of England, it was believed that the ghosts of all persons who were destined to die in the coming year could be seen walking through the grave-yards at midnight on Samhain. Many of the ghosts were thought to be evil, and so for protection, jack-o'lanterns with hideous candle-lit faces were carved out of pumpkins and carried as lanterns to scare away the malevolent spirits. In Scotland, the traditional Hallows jack-o'lantern was carved out of turnips.

An old Belgian Samhain custom was to prepare special "Cakes for the Dead" (small white cakes or cookies). A cake was eaten for each spirit honored with the belief that the more cakes you ate, the more the dead would bless you!

Another old Samhain custom was to light a fire on the household hearth which would burn continuously until the first day of the following spring. Huge bonfires were also lit on the hilltops at sunset in honor of the old

Gods and Goddesses, and to guide the souls of the dead home to their kin.

It was on Samhain that the Celtic Druids tallied their livestock and mated their ewes for the coming Spring. Surplus breeding stock were sacrificed to the Gods and wicker effegies of people and horses were burned as offerings.

It is said that lighting a new orange candle at midnight on Samhain and allowing it to burn until sunrise will bring one good luck; however, according to an old legend, bad luck will befall those who bake bread on this day or journey after sunset.

The divinatory arts of scrying (crystal-gazing) and rune-casting on the magickal night of Samhain are Wiccan traditions, as is standing before a mirror and making a secret wish.

Samhain Sabbat Ritual

It is traditional to fast for a whole day before performing the Samhain Sabbat Rite.

After a ritual bath in salt water to cleanse the soul of all impurities, put on a long, white ceremonial robe (unless you prefer to work sky-clad, as many Witches do), wear a necklace of acorns around your neck and an oak leaf crown around your head.

Cast a circle about nine feet in diameter, using white chalk or paint. Place 13 black and orange candles around the circle and as you light each one, say:

> SAMHAIN CANDLE OF FIRE SO BRIGHT
> CONSECRATE THIS CIRCLE OF LIGHT.

In the center of the consecrated circle, erect an altar facing north. On the center of the altar, place three white candles. (One to represent each phase of the Triple Goddess.) To the left (west), place a chalice filled with apple cider. To the right (east), place a censer of herb incense. Before the candles (south), place an altar bell, a consecrated athame and an apple.

Ring the altar bell thrice. Take the athame in your right hand and say:

> HEARKEN WELL YE ELEMENTS
> AIR, FIRE, WATER, EARTH
> BY BELL AND BLADE I SUMMON THEE
> ON THIS SACRED NIGHT OF MIRTH.

Light the incense and the three white altar candles and say:

THREE CANDLES OF SACRED WHITE
I DO LIGHT IN HONOR OF THEE, O GODDESS.
ONE FOR THE MAIDEN
ONE FOR THE MOTHER
ONE FOR THE CRONE.

O GODDESS OF ALL THINGS WILD AND FREE,
STRONG AND LOVING, FAIR AND JUST,
THIS SACRED TEMPLE I RAISE TO THEE
IN PERFECT LOVE, IN PERFECT TRUST.

Take the athame in your right hand and dip the blade into the chalice as you say:

I OFFER TO THEE, O GODDESS
THIS NECTAR OF THE SEASON.

Return the athame to the altar. Pick up the chalice with both hands and pour a few drops of the cider onto the apple and say:

BLESSED BE THE SOULS OF THOSE
WHO HAVE JOURNEYED BEYOND
TO THE DARK WORLD OF THE DEAD.
I POUR THIS NECTAR
IN HONOR OF THEIR MEMORY.
MAY THE GODS BLESS THEM
WITH LIGHT, BEAUTY AND JOY.
BLESSED BE!
BLESSED BE!

Drink the remaining cider and then return the chalice to its place on the altar. Ring the bell three times and then uncast the circle by putting out the orange and black candles, starting in the east and moving in a counter-clockwise direction.

Take the apple from the altar and bury it outside in the earth to nourish the souls of those who have died in the past year.

The ritual is now complete and should be followed by meditation, divination by crystal ball, and/or the reciting of mystical Goddess-inspired poetry.

Spring Equinox Sabbat

The Spring Equinox Sabbat (also known as Ostara, the Rite of Eostre) celebrates the birth of Spring and pays homage to the fertility goddess Eostre.

Like most of the Christian holidays, Easter (which celebrates the resurrection of Christ just days after the Vernal Equinox) is rich with an abundance of Pagan overtones, customs and traditions.

Easter originally marked the springtime sacrificial festival named after the Saxon fertility goddess Eostre, or Ostara. The holiday was not officially given the name of the goddess until the end of the Middle Ages.

To this day, Easter Sunday is determined by the ancient lunar calander system which places the holiday on the first Sunday following the Vernal Spring Equinox. (Formally, this marked the "pregnant" phase of the Goddess passing into the fertile season.)

The Easter Bunny is actually the Moon Hare sacred to many of the lunar goddesses in both Western and Eastern cultures. The hare as a fertility symbol represents rebirth and resurrection.

The coloring of Easter eggs is also an ancient Pagan custom associated with Eostre. Eggs, which are obvious symbols of fertility and reproduction, were decorated with magickal symbols and used in fertility rituals as offerings to the Goddess. Eggs were also painted yellow or gold (sacred solar colors) and used in ritual in honor of the Sun God.

Spring Sabbat Ritual

(Rite of Eostre)

Cast a circle about nine feet in diameter. Erect an altar in the center of the circle facing north.

Place a light green candle on the middle of the altar. To the right (east) of the candle, place a censer of jasmine incense or a thurible containing a hot charcoal block whereupon sage can be burned. To the left (west) of the candle, place a bowl of hard-boiled eggs decorated with runes, fertility designs and other magickal symbols. Before the candle (south), place a consecrated athame and a ceremonial sword.

After sprinkling a bit of salt on the circle, take the ceremonial sword and trace the circle in a clockwise motion, starting in the east. As you trace the circle, say:

BLESSED BE THIS SABBAT CIRCLE
IN THE DIVINE NAME OF EOSTRE
ANCIENT GODDESS OF FERTILITY.

Return the sword to the altar and then light the candle and incense. Take the athame in your right hand and kneel before the altar with the blade of the athame held over your heart and say:

BLESSED BE THE FERTILITY GODDESS,
BLESSED BE HER SPRINGTIME RITE.
BLESSED BE THE SUN GOD-KING,
BLESSED BE HIS SACRED LIGHT.

Place the blade of the athame over your forehead (third eye) and say:

> THE SUN HAS CROSSED
> THE CELESTIAL EQUATOR
> GIVING SUN AND MOON EQUAL HOURS.
> GODDESS SPRING IS REBORN AGAIN
> HER BEAUTY GIVES LIFE
> TO THE TREES AND FLOWERS.
>
> BLESSED BE THE GODDESS OF LIFE:
> BLESSED BE THE LADY OF LIGHT:
> SHE IS THE CREATRESS OF ALL
>   LIVING THINGS.
>
> THE GODDESS BREATHES LIFE
> THE GODDESS GIVES LIFE
> THE GODDESS IS LIFE
> THE GODDESS REIGNS SUPREME
> SO MOTE IT BE!

End the rite by putting out the candle and uncasting the circle with the ceremonial sword in a counter-clockwise motion.

The eggs may be eaten as part of a Spring Equinox Sabbat feast and the shells buried in the ground as an offering to the Earth Mother.

Summer Solstice

(Midsummer)

Summer Solstice marks the longest day of the year when the sun is at its zenith. For Witches, this day symbolizes the power of the sun which marks an important turning point on the Great Wheel of the Year, for after the Solstice of Summer, the days grow visibly shorter.

In certain Wiccan traditions, the Summer Solstice (also known as Litha) symbolizes the end of the reign of the Oak-King who is now replaced by his successor the Holly-King who will rule until the Sabbat of Yule, the shortest day of the year.

Midsummer is the traditional time when Witches harvest magickal herbs for spells and potions, for it is believed that the innate power of herbs are strongest on this day.

Summer Solstice Rite

The following ritual should be performed in a forest clearing, a large secluded garden, on a hilltop, or any other nature place.

Arrange stones on the ground to form a large circle about nine feet in diameter. With a consecrated ceremonial sword or long wooden stick, draw the powerful symbol of a pentacle (five-pointed star) inside the stone circle. Light five green candles to symbolize nature and fertility and place one at each point of the pentagram, starting at the east point and continuing in a clockwise manner.

Lay a large, flat stone in the center of the pentagram facing north as an altar and place on it a statue representing the Goddess. At each side of the statue, light a white altar candle. To the right (east), place a brass bell and a censer of frankincense and myrrh incense. To the left (west), place a chalice of wine, a consecrated brass bell, a small dish of salt, and a small bowl of water.

Bless the wine by holding your palms down over the chalice as you say:

I CONSECRATE AND BLESS THIS WINE
IN THE DIVINE NAME OF THE GODDESS.

Sprinkle a bit of salt and a few drops of water over the brass bell to consecrate it and say:

WITH SALT AND WATER
I CONSECRATE AND BLESS THIS BELL
IN THE DIVINE NAME OF THE GODDESS.
BLESSED BE.

Light the frankincense and myrrh. Raise your arms to the sky, close your eyes and fill your mind with pleasant thoughts and visions of the Mother Goddess as you say:

O BLESSED EARTH MOTHER
WOMB-GODDESS, CREATRESS OF ALL
THIS SACRED CIRCLE IS CONSECRATED
TO THEE.

Ring the bell thrice and invoke:

SACRED LADYSPIRIT OF THE AIR
FIRE MAIDEN, BEAUTIFUL AND FAIR
EARTH MOTHER, GIVER OF LIVES
CRONE OF WATER, AGELESS AND WISE
I NOW CALL FORTH THY DIVINE IMAGE!

Return the bell to the stone altar and then with both hands, raise the chalice to your lips. Drink some of the wine and then pour the rest over the center of the pentagram as a libation to the Goddess and say:

> THIS BLESSED WINE I DO POUR
> AS AN OFFERING TO THEE
> O GRACIOUS GODDESS.

Return the chalice to the altar. Again ring the bell thrice and say:

> THIS SOLSTICE RITUAL I DO PERFORM
> IN HONOR OF THEE, O GREAT GODDESS
> AND IN THY SACRED NAME
> DO I NOW GIVE PRAISE.

Kneel before the altar. Offer up more incense, ring the bell in praise of the Goddess and then say in a loud and joyous tone of voice:

> BLESSED BE THE GODDESS!
> BLESSED BE THE GODDESS!
>
> THE GODDESS IS LIFE
> THE GODDESS IS LOVE
> SHE TURNS THE WHEEL
> THAT CHANGES THE SEASONS
> AND BRINGS NEW LIFE INTO THE WORLD.
>
> BLESSED BE THE GODDESS!
> BLESSED BE THE GODDESS!
>
> THE GODDESS IS THE MOON AND STARS
> THE GODDESS IS THE SEA AND EARTH
> THE GODDESS IS THE CYCLE OF SEASONS
> SHE IS BIRTH, SHE IS DEATH
> SHE IS RE-BIRTH.

SHE IS DAY, SHE IS NIGHT
SHE IS DARKNESS, SHE IS LIGHT
SHE IS ALL THINGS WILD AND FREE
SO MOTE IT BE.

The Rite of the Summer Solstice should be followed by feasting, merriment and the joyous singing of magickal Pagan folk songs.

Autumn Equinox

The Autumn Equinox Sabbat is the second festival of Harvest. It is the time to celebrate the completion of the grain harvest which began at Lammas, and to pay homage to the Great Horned God.

Many Wiccan traditions perform a rite for the Goddess Persephone's descent into the Underworld as part of their Autumn Equinox celebration. According to myth, on the day of the Equinox, Hades, the Lord of the Underworld, came upon Persephone who was picking flowers. He was so taken by her youthful beauty that he instantly fell in love with her. He snatched her up and carried her off to the darkness of his domain to eternally rule by his side as his immortal Queen of the Underworld. Goddess Demeter's sorrow for her stolen daughter was so intense that she caused the flowers and the leaves of the trees to wither and die.

Autumn Equinox Sabbat Ritual

Cast a circle about nine feet in diameter. In the center, erect an altar facing north. On the altar, place an orange candle, a consecrated athame, a dish of salt, a consecrated altar bell and a censer of incense. (The following incenses are sacred on this Sabbat: benzoin, myrrh, passion-flower, red poppies and sage.)

Decorate the altar with traditional holiday decorations: acorns, pinecones, marigolds, white roses and thistles. The flowers can be arranged in bouquets or garlands for the altar or made into a crown and worn on top of the head.

Consecrate the circle with salt in the usual manner and say:

> WITH SACRED SALT
> I CONSECRATE THIS SABBAT CIRCLE.
> SO MOTE IT BE.

Light the candle and incense. Take the altar bell in your left hand and ring it thrice to begin the equinox rite and conjuration of the elements. Take the athame in your right hand, face the east and say:

> O SACRED SYLPHS OF THE AIR
> AND ELEMENTAL KINGS OF THE EAST
> I CONJURE THEE AND BID YE TO
> COME AND PARTAKE IN THIS HOLY SABBAT
> IN THIS CONSECRATED CIRCLE.
> SO MOTE IT BE.

Ring the altar bell thrice. Face the south and say:

O SACRED SALAMANDERS OF THE FIRE
AND ELEMENTAL KINGS OF THE SOUTH
I CONJURE THEE AND BID YE TO
COME AND PARTAKE IN THIS HOLY SABBAT
IN THIS CONSECRATED CIRCLE.
SO MOTE IT BE.

Ring the altar bell thrice. Face the west and say:

O SACRED UNDINES OF THE WATER
AND ELEMENTAL KINGS OF THE WEST
I CONJURE THEE AND BID YE TO
COME AND PARTAKE IN THIS HOLY SABBAT
IN THIS CONSECRATED CIRCLE.
SO MOTE IT BE.

Ring the altar bell thrice. Face the north and say:

O SACRED GNOMES OF THE EARTH
AND ELEMENTAL KINGS OF THE NORTH
I CONJURE THEE AND BID YE TO
COME AND PARTAKE IN THIS HOLY SABBAT
IN THIS CONSECRATED CIRCLE
SO MOTE IT BE.

Return the bell and athame to the altar. Stand with
your arms stretched out before you and say:

AIR, FIRE, WATER, EARTH
WOMB TO LIFE, DEATH TO RE-BIRTH.
THE GREAT WHEEL OF THE SEASONS TURNS,
THE SACRED SABBAT FIRE BURNS.
WE ARE ALL CHILDREN OF THE GODDESS
AND TO HER WE SHALL RETURN.

Ring the altar bell thrice and say:

O GREAT GODDESS
EARTH MOTHER OF ALL LIVING THINGS
WE BID THEE FAREWELL
AS YE GO NOW TO REST.
BLESSED BE.

AND WE WELCOME THEE
O GREAT HORNED GOD OF THE HUNT,
EARTH FATHER OF ALL LIVING THINGS.
BLESSED BE.

Ring the altar bell thrice to end the rite and then uncast the circle.

Winter Solstice Sabbat (Yule)

Winter Solstice is the longest night of the year, and it is on this night when Witches honor the darkness and the Great Horned God who rules the dark half of the year.

The modern day customs that are associated with the Christian religious holiday of Christmas, such as decorating the tree, hanging mistletoe and holly and burning the Yule log, are all beautiful Pagan customs that date back to pre-Christian times when the Witches' Sabbat of Yule (which takes place on the Winter Solstice just days before Christmas) originally commemorated the re-birth of the Sun God.

The burning of the Yule log stems from the ancient custom of the Yule bonfire which was burned to give life and power to the sun, which was thought of as being reborn at the Winter Solstice. In later times, the outdoor bonfire custom was replaced by the indoor burning of logs and red candles etched with carvings of suns and other magickal symbols. As the oak tree was considered to be the Cosmic Tree of the ancient Druids, the Yule log is traditionally oak. Other Wiccan traditions use a pine Yule log to symbolize the dying god Attis, Dionysus or Woden. At the end of the year, the log is ritually burned to mark the death of winter and the rebirth of the sun. In days of old, the ashes of the Yule log were mixed with cow fodder to aid in symbolic reproduction and was sprinkled over the fields to insure new life and a fertile spring.

Another favorite Christmas tradition rich in Pagan symbolism is the hanging of mistletoe in doorways. Mistletoe was considered very magickal by the ancient Druids who called it the "Golden Bough." They believed that it possessed great healing powers and gave men access to the Underworld. The living plant, which is actually a parasite, at one time has been thought of as the genitalia of the god Zeus, whose sacred tree is the oak. The phallic significance of mistletoe stems from the idea that its white berries were drops of the God's divine semen in contrast to the red berries of the holly which were equated with the sacred menstrual blood of the Goddess. The life-giving essence which the mistletoe suggests provides a symbolic divine substance and a sense of immortality to those who hang it at Yuletide. The modern custom of kissing under the mistletoe is just a pale shadow of the sexual orgies that once accompanied the rites of the oak god.

The Christmas tree custom evolved from the pine groves associated with the Great Mother Goddess. The lights and ornaments hung on the tree as decorations are actually symbols of the sun, moon and stars as they appear in the Cosmic Tree of Life. They also represent departed souls who are remembered at the end of the year. Sacred presents (Christmas gifts) were also hung on the tree as offerings to various deities such as Attis and Dionysus.

Even jolly old Kris Kringle (Santa Claus) was at one time the Pagan god of Yule. He was known as "Christ on the Wheel," an ancient Norse title for the Sun God who was reborn at the Winter Solstice.

Placing cakes in the boughs of the oldest apple trees in the orchard and pouring on cider as a libation was an old Pagan Yuletide custom practiced in England and known as "Wassailing the Orchard Trees." It was said that the cider was a substitute for the human or animal blood offered in earlier times as part of a Winter Solstice fertility rite. After offering a toast to the health of the apple trees and giving thanks to them for producing fruit, the farmers would then enjoin the trees to continue producing abundantly.

Winter Solstice/Yule Sabbat Ritual

Erect an altar, facing north. Around it, cast a circle about nine feet in diameter using white chalk or paint. Decorate the circle with holly and/or mistletoe.

Place a white altar candle on the center of the altar. To the left of the candle, place a chalice of red wine or apple cider and a censer of incense. (Any of the following incense fragrances are appropriate for this ritual: bay, cedar, pine or rosemary.) To the right of the candle, place an athame and a dash of salt. Behind the altar, place an oak log with 13 green and red candles affixed to it.

Take the athame in your right hand and scoop up a bit of salt with the tip of the blade. Drop the salt from the athame onto the circle. Repeat three times and say:

BLESSED BE THIS SACRED CIRCLE
IN THE NAME OF THE
  GREAT HORNED GOD
THE DIVINE LORD OF DARKNESS
  AND LIGHT
THE GOD OF DEATH AND ALL THAT
  COMES AFTER
BLESSED BE THIS SACRED CIRCLE
  IN HIS NAME.

Place the athame on the left side of the altar, next to the chalice. After lighting the incense and altar candle, take the athame in your left hand, dip the blade into the chalice, and say:

WATER, AIR, FIRE, EARTH
WE CELEBRATE THE SUN'S RE-BIRTH

ON THIS DARK AND LONGEST NIGHT
WE BURN THE SACRED CANDLES BRIGHT.

Return the athame to its place on the altar. Pick up the chalice with both hands and, as you raise it to your lips, say:

THIS WINE I DRINK TO HONOR THEE
O GOD OF ALL THINGS WILD AND FREE.

Drink the wine and then return the chalice to the altar. Light the 13 candles on the Yule log and end the rite by saying:

WE THANK THEE FOR THE LIGHT OF THE SUN
HAIL TO THEE, O GREAT HORNED ONE.
SO MOTE IT BE.

Celebrate merrily and feast with family and friends until the last candle on the Yule log burns itself out.

6

Candle Magick

Magick

"Magick is the art, science and practice of causing change to occur in conformity and control events in nature with will." (As a tool of Witchcraft, the old spelling of the word with the "K" at the end is used to distinguish it from the magic of theatrical stage conjuring and illusion.)

In order to work magick properly, a Witch or magician must be in perfect harmony with the laws of nature and the psyche. It is important to possess magickal knowledge, mental concentration, a healthy body and mind, and the ability to accept responsibility for one's own actions.

Positive results cannot be magickally achieved if the person attempting to perform the spell has a low energy level, lacks confidence or conviction, or contaminates his or her body with drugs and/or alcohol.

Moon Magick: The Lunar Phases

It is extremely important that magick spells and rituals be performed during the proper lunar phase of the moon.

A Waxing Moon (the time from the new moon through the first quarter to the full moon) is the proper time to perform positive magick and spells that increase love, sexual desire, good luck and wealth.

A Full Moon increases extrasensory perception and is the proper time to perform lunar Goddess invocations, fertility rituals and spells that increase psychic abilities and prophetic dreams.

A Waning Moon (the time from the full moon through the last quarter to the new moon) is the proper time to perform destructive magick, negative incantations, and spells that remove curses, hexes and jinxes, end bad relationships, reverse love spells, break bad habits and decrease fevers, pains and sickness.

The Wiccan Rede

Before performing any magick spells or rituals, it is very important that you keep in mind the Wiccan Rede: "AN IT HARM NONE, DO WHAT THOU WILT." Do your own thing, as long as it doesn't harm anybody.

The Threefold Law

If you use White Magick (positive) to do good, three times the good will come back to you. If you use Black Magick (negative) to do evil, the evil will also return to you threefold.

Self-Dedication Ritual

(for Solitary Witches)

On a night of the full moon, cast a circle with white chalk or paint, about six feet in diameter. Sprinkle a bit of salt over the circle to consecrate it.

Sit in the center of the circle facing north with two white candles and a censer of frankincense and myrrh incense before you. (It is best to perform this ritual sky-clad [nude]; however, if you feel uncomfortable working without clothes, you may wear a white ceremonial robe instead.)

Light the incense and meditate for awhile until your mind is free of all unpleasant thoughts and your body is completely relaxed. Light the first candle and say:

> O MOTHER GODDESS, CREATRESS OF LIFE
> IN THIS SACRED CIRCLE OF LIGHT
> I DO PLEDGE MYSELF TO HONOR AND
>   SERVE THEE
> AND TO ABIDE BY THY WICCAN REDE
> FOR AS LONG AS I SHALL LIVE.
> SO MOTE IT BE.

Light the second candle and say:

> O GREAT HORNED GOD, LORD OF THE
>   WOODLANDS
> IN THIS SACRED CIRCLE OF LIGHT
> I DO PLEDGE MYSELF TO HONOR
>   AND SERVE THEE
> AND TO PROTECT THE SECRETS
>   OF THE ANCIENT ONES

FOR AS LONG AS I SHALL LIVE.
SO MOTE IT BE.

Hold your open hands up to the sky. Close your eyes and visualize two white beams of glowing light streaking down from the heavens above and flowing into your palms. A warm, tingling feeling will begin to spread throughout your body as the love power of the Goddess and God cleanses your soul of all evil and negativity.

Remain in the circle until both of the candles have burned themselves out.

Planetary Rulers & Ritual Influences of the Days of the Week

SUNDAY (ruled by the Sun) is the proper day of the week to perform spells and rituals involving exorcism, healing and prosperity. *Colors*: orange, white, yellow. *Incense*: frankincense, lemon.

MONDAY (ruled by the Moon) is the proper day of the week to perform spells and rituals involving agriculture, animals, female fertility, messages, reconciliation, theft and voyages. *Colors*: silver, white, gray. *Incense*: African violet, honeysuckle, myrtle, willow, wormwood.

TUESDAY (ruled by Mars) is the proper day of the week to perform spells and rituals involving courage, physical strength, revenge, military honors, surgery and the breaking of negative spells. *Colors*: red, orange. *Incense*: dragon's blood, patchouly.

WEDNESDAY (ruled by Mercury) is the proper day of the week to perform spells and rituals involving communication, divination, writing, knowledge and business transactions. *Colors*: yellow, gray, violet, and all opalescent hues. *Incense*: jasmine, lavender, sweetpea.

THURSDAY (ruled by Jupiter) is the proper day of the week to perform spells and rituals involving luck, happiness, health, legal matters, male fertility, treasure and wealth. *Colors*: blue, purple, indigo. *Incense*: cinnamon, musk, nutmeg, sage.

FRIDAY (ruled by Venus) is the proper day of the week to perform spells and rituals involving love, romance, beauty, sex, marriage, friendships and partnerships. *Colors*: pink, green, aqua, chartreuse. *Incense*: strawberry, sandalwood, rose, saffron, vanilla.

SATURDAY (ruled by Saturn) is the proper day of the week to perform spells and rituals involving spirit communication, meditation, psychic attack or defense and locating lost things or missing persons. *Colors*: black, gray, indigo. *Incense*: black poppy seeds, myrrh.

Magick Secrets for Making Oneself Beloved

To make oneself beloved, according to a Medieval Grimoire, put a dead frog in an earthen vessel full of small holes and place it on top of an anthill. After the ants have eaten away the frog's skin and flesh, grind its skeleton into a fine powder. Mix it with the blood of a bat and then throw a pinch of it into the food or drink of the person from whom you desire love.

A love philtre from the Middle Ages: Take the heart of a dove, the liver of a sparrow, the womb of a swallow and the kidney of a hare and reduce them to a fine powder. To the philtre add an equal part of your blood, also dried and powdered. When the moon is in Venus, put some of the love powder into the food or drink of the person whom you desire, and after they swallow it, they shall be drawn into love.

A modern Witch's love philtre calls for passion flowers, patchouly leaves, basil, cloves and sweet red wine. The herbs are powdered and mixed together by the light of a red (or pink) candle and put into the wine which is then given to the intended lover to drink.

It is very important to remember when preparing philtres or casting love spells to always concentrate on the man or woman whose affections you desire. Chant his or her name over and over as you work your magick and visualize yourself and that person as passionate lovers. Creative visualization is the key to successful magick!

To make the person you love want to marry you, gather an Adam and Eve root on St. John's Eve and powder it by the light of the moon. Mix it with some sand and a few drops of blood from the ring finger of your left hand. Write your name in the sand mixture and then, when the time is right, sprinkle a bit of it in the hair of the intended spouse.

To gain a prophetic dream of one's future true love, recite these words as you pluck a sprig of the mystical ash tree:

> EVEN ASH, EVEN ASH
> I PLUCK THEE,
> THIS NIGHT MY TRUE LOVE
> FOR TO SEE.

The Willow Knot Spell

To win the love of a girl, according to old Gypsy Witch lore, a young man must go into the woods and find some willow twigs that have grown together into a knot. With a sharp, white-handled knife, he must cut the twigs, put them into his mouth and repeat the following words with his eyes closed:

> WILLOW TREE, WILLOW TREE
> GIVE ME THE LUCK OF THINE,
> THEN (name of loved one) SHALT BE MINE.

Candle Love Spell

To make a man desire you, write his name with yours nine times on a pink candle. Anoint the candle with a mixture of rose water and honey and allow the candle to burn every night for nine nights in a row.

Ancient Gypsy Love Spell

Plant an onion or garlic in a red clay pot, and as you plant it, repeat the name of the man or woman whom you desire love from. Everyday at sunrise and sunset you must water the plant and recite the following magickal spell:

> AS THIS ROOT GROWS
> LET THE HEART OF (name)
> BE TURNED UNTO ME.

Spell to Cure Impotency

(Perform this powerful spell when the moon is in Scorpio—the sign of the zodiac which influences the sexual organs.)

Place an old iron key and a piece of dragon's blood resin beneath the mattress and chant:

IRON KEY TO UNLOCK DESIRE,
DRAGON'S BLOOD FOR PASSION FIRE,
O LUNAR GODDESS OF THE SCORPION MOON
LET SEXUAL ENERGY FILL THIS ROOM!

Place three crimson-red candles on the floor: one at each side of the bed and one at the foot of the bed. Light the candles and burn musk, jasmine or vanilla incense to infuse the bedroom with sexual vibrations. Sprinkle pink rose petals on the sheets, fill your mind with erotic thoughts, and then make love with your sexual partner.

Incantation Against Disease

On a night of the New Moon, take a piece of white chalk and draw a pentacle (five-pointed star) on the floor about four feet wide. Light a white candle and hold it in your right hand. Step into the pentacle, face east and thrice recite the following incantation of Albertus Magnus:

OFANO
OBLAMO
OSPERGO
HOLA NOA
MASSA LUX BEFF
CLEMATI ADONAI
CLEONA FLORIT
PAX SAX SARAX
AFA AFACA NOSTRA
CERUM HEAIUM
LADA FRIUM

Magick Charm Triangles

1. For protection against evil spirits, light a white candle and write the following Gnostic charm triangle on parchment, using Witches' ink made from an acorn of a valonia oak tree. Carry the charm with you in your right pocket:

```
A B L A N A T H A N A L B A
  B L A N A T H A N A L B
    L A N A T H A N A L
      A N A T H A N A
        N A T H A N
          A T H A
            T H
```

2. To banish fever from man or beast, light a blue candle and write the following Gypsy charm triangle in blood on an onion skin, which is then burned and the ashes rubbed on the forehead of the feverish person or animal:

```
O C H N O T I N O S
  C H N O T I N O
    H N O T I N
      N O T I
        O T
```

The Red Cord Spell

Take a red cord about 12 inches long and tie four knots in it, uttering these words as you go along:

ONE KNOT FOR LUCK
TWO KNOTS FOR WEALTH
THREE KNOTS FOR LOVE
FOUR KNOTS FOR HEALTH

Burn the cord at midnight on St. John's Eve and place the ashes in a small red bag along with a sprig of rue, a morsel of bread, three cumin seeds and a pinch of sea salt. Sew the bag shut with red thread and then recite the following incantation:

I SEW THIS BAG FOR LUCK AND WEALTH
WITH STRING OF RED FOR LOVE AND HEALTH
THAT IT MAY KEEP BY NIGHT AND DAY
WOE AND SICKNESS FAR AWAY.

Bury the bag in a flower pot and keep it on a window facing east.

Magick Handbell

Before the dawning of Spiritualism in the early 19th century, necromancers used a special bell with mysterious powers as a magickal tool to evoke the spirits of the dead.

To make a magick handbell, also known as "the necromantic bell of Girardius," the metals of copper, gold, iron, lead, silver, tin and fixed mercury must be cast together at the day and hour of the birth of the magician who is to make use of the bell. Inscribe the name ADONAI on or below the handle of the bell; above the rim of the bell, inscribe the divine name TETRAGRAM-MATON; and between the two names of power, inscribe the magician's date of birth along with the names of the seven planetary spirits: ARATRON, BETHOR, PHALEG, OCH, HAGITH, OPHIEL, PHUEL.

After inscribing the handbell, consecrate it with water and salt, wrap it in a piece of green taffeta and put it into the middle of a grave in a cemetery for seven days and nights.

To make the spirit of a dead person appear before you at your command, trace a large magick circle within a circle over the dead person's grave. Stand in the center of the inner circle with wand held in right hand and bell in left hand. Tap the wand on the ground thrice and say:

RAPHAEL, RAEL, REX
RAPHAEL, RAEL REX
TETRAGRAMMATON
ADONAI

Ring the magick handbell thrice and repeat the incantation to summon the spirit.

Mojo Bags

A mojo bag is a small flannel or leather drawstring bag (usually three inches wide and four inches long) that is filled with various magickal items and carried or worn as a charm to attract or dispel certain influences.

FOR PROTECTION AGAINST THE EVIL EYE, put the following magickal things into a mojo bag: a piece of coral, a clove of garlic, St. John's wort, a white feather and the lucky birth-charm of the person for whom the bag is made. (See the list of lucky birth-charms immediately following the Mojo spells.) Light a dark blue candle and charge and mojo bag with powder by anointing it with a few drops of oil and thrice repeating this chant:

> WITH POWER OF PROTECTION
> I NOW CHARGE THEE.
> KAYN AYN HORAH
> SO MOTE IT BE!

TO BANISH SICKNESS FROM MAN OR BEAST, light a white candle on a night of the new moon and fill a mojo bag with the lucky birth-charm of the person for whom the bag is made along with the following healing herbs: angelica, bay leaves, cinnamon, fennel seeds, horehound, rose petals, rosemary, thyme, vervain and violet flowers. Tie the bag with a white string, anoint it with oil and say:

> WITCHES' HERBS AND MAGICK FLOWERS
> FILL THIS BAG WITH HEALING POWER.
> LET THE WEARER OF THIS CHARM
> BE FREE OF SICKNESS, PAIN AND HARM.
> SO MOTE IT BE!

TO BREAK THE POWER OF AN EVIL SPELL OR CURSE AND TURN THE BLACK MAGICK BACK UPON THE INSTIGATOR, light a black candle on a Saturday at the first hour of sunset and fill a mojo bag with a bit of dirt from a new grave, a coffin nail, the powdered skull of a toad, a pinch of brimstone, three rusty pins and something belonging to your "enemy," such as his or her fingernail clippings, a lock of hair, a photograph or even threads from his or her clothing. Tie the bag with a black string and anoint the outer edges of the bag with a small amount of oil. Place both of your hands over the bag and chant thrice the following incantation:

GOD AND GODDESS, HEAR MY VERSE
MOJO MAGICK LIFT THIS CURSE
AND SEND THE EVIL BACK TO HE/SHE
WHO WISHES ME HARM. SO MOTE IT BE!

Place the mojo bag under the front steps of the enemy's house or hang it from a tree near the front door so that the wicked person's aura will absorb the negative energy from the mojo bag every time he or she passes by it.

TO MAKE A MOJO LOVE BAG, place your lucky birth-charm and the birth-charm of your intended lover together in a mojo bag with some basil (the herb of love), catnip, rosebuds and serpentaria root. Tie the bag shut with a pink string, light a red or pink candle and anoint the bag with a small amount of oil as you say:

BLESSED BE THIS CHARM OF LOVE
WITH GODDESS POWER FROM ABOVE.
SO MOTE IT BE!

Lucky Birth-Charms

Each astrological sign of the zodiac rules one or more gemstone, known as a birth-charm.

Birth-charms are used in mojo charm bags or worn as magickal jewelry to attract good luck, love or health, and to protect against evil, illness and misfortune; however, it is considered extremely unlucky to wear a birth-charm belonging to an astrological sign other than your own.

According to the astrologically-minded magicians of the Middle Ages, a birth-charm must be made or purchased on the appropriate day of the week, otherwise the gemstone will be powerless. It is also very important that the hour in which it is made or purchased be either 8:00 A.M., 3:00 P.M., or 1:00 A.M. (These are the hours when the planet of the day is most influential.)

The following is an alphabetical list of lucky birth-charms, their astrological and planetary correspondents, and the days of the week which influence them:

Agate	Gemini (Mercury)	Wednesday
Amber	Leo (Sun)	Sunday
Amethyst	Aquarius (Saturn/Uranus)	Saturday
Aquamarine	Pisces (Jupiter/Neptune)	Thursday
Bloodstone	Leo (Sun)	Sunday
Carnelian	Taurus (Venus)	Friday
Coral	Aries (Mars)	Tuesday
Diamond	Aries (Mars)	Tuesday
Emerald	Taurus (Venus)	Friday
Garnet	Capricorn (Saturn)	Saturday
Jacinth	Aquarius (Saturn/Uranus)	Saturday
Jade	Libra (Venus)	Friday
Lapis Lazuli	Pisces (Jupiter/Neptune)	Thursday
Malachite	Taurus (Venus)	Friday

Moonstone	Cancer (Moon)	Monday
Obsidian	Capricorn (Saturn)	Saturday
Onyx	Capricorn (Saturn)	Saturday
Opal	Libra (Venus)	Friday
Pearl	Cancer (Moon)	Monday
Quartz Crystal	Aquarius (Saturn/Uranus)	Saturday
Ruby	Leo (Sun)	Sunday
Sapphire	Virgo (Mercury)	Wednesday
Sardonyx	Virgo (Mercury)	Wednesday
Topaz	Scorpio (Mars/Pluto)	Tuesday
Tourmaline	Libra (Venus)	Friday
Turquoise	Sagittarius (Jupiter)	Thursday

Prophetic Dream Spell

To conjure forth a prophetic dream, perform this spell on a night when the moon is full and in the sign of the Water Bearer or the Scorpion. (For best results it is advisable to fast with water for one whole day before performing this spell.)

Into a cauldron (or large kettle) of boiling water throw a pinch each of white sand, powdered cat's eye (gemstone) and some old chimney soot. Grind and mix together a small quantity of St. John's Wort, frankincense, adder's tongue and mandrake root. Add three tablespoons of the ground-up herbal mixture to the cauldron water and stir it thoroughly with a large wooden spoon as you recite the following magickal rhyme:

ST. JOHN'S WORT GATHERED BY NIGHT
FRANKINCENSE AND SAND OF WHITE
ADDER'S TONGUE AND MANDRAKE ROOT
CAT'S EYE POWDERED AND CHIMNEY SOOT
I MIX TOGETHER IN THIS CAULDRON OF STEAM
TO CONJURE FORTH A PROPHETIC DREAM.

Let the mixture bubble for awhile and then remove the cauldron from the fire. After it has cooled, draw a bath and add a few drops of the brew to the bathwater. Light a purple candle and place it near the tub. Remove your clothes and soak your body in the relaxing herbal bath as you gaze into the flame of the candle. Open your heart and mind to the Goddess and chant her name either out loud or telepathically until you feel her divine presence enter you.

After bathing, wrap your body in a white or purple robe, sprinkle a bit of the brew in a circle around your bed and say:

> I CONSECRATE THIS DREAM CIRCLE
> IN THE NAME OF THE GODDESS.
> BLESSED BE!

Now sprinkle a bit of the brew upon your pillow and then lay yourself down to sleep. Before the rising of the sun, you will experience one or more prophetic dreams.

Treasure Spell

In the witching hour of Saint John's night
a blazing fire ye must light
to spark a brew that's vile and strong
as ye heed this magickal song:

In a cauldron mix together
purple heather and black bird's feather,
root of mandrake, heart of lizard,
lock of hair from a sleeping wizard,
powdered cat's eye, blood of dragon,
wing of flittermouse, horn of stag, and
let the brew for three nights sit,
stir with wand, then in it spit
twice for luck, thrice for good measure.
Come next morn, be rich with treasure!

(PLEASE NOTE: "Powdered cat's eye" is a gemstone
and not the powdered eye of a cat: "Blood of dragon" refers to Dragon's Blood: a red, resinous substance obtained from the fruit of a tree,
Daemonorops draco, of tropical Asia. A "flittermouse" is, of course, a bat.)

Weatherworking

TO BRING RAIN IN TIMES OF DROUGHT, cast a circle in the parched earth, using a consecrated ceremonial sword or wand. Sprinkle a bit of salt and water over the circle to clear it of any negative or evil forces. Draw a pentacle inside the circle and place a blue candle at each point of the star. Light the candles and then burn 13 ferns in the center of the star and chant:

RAIN COME HITHER, LORD ADAD
   COMMANDS THEE
RAIN COME HITHER, LORD BAAL
   COMMANDS THEE
RAIN COME HITHER, LORD ILYAPA
   COMMANDS THEE
RAIN COME HITHER, LORD THUNOR
COMMANDS THEE
RAIN COME HITHER, LORD ZEUS
   COMMANDS THEE
SO MOTE IT BE!

As you sing the chant, visualize rainclouds gathering above and rain falling from the sky to the earth. Continue chanting and concentrating on the visualization until you feel energy building up within you, and then direct the power into the earth to energize the region to attract rain.

After the rain comes, spiritually express your thanks to the Gods and then uncast the circle. (Please note: When performing weather magick, results may take up to several days or they may be immediate. It is also important to keep in mind that weatherworking should only be done in extreme emergencies for it can be ecologically dangerous to tamper with the delicate balance of forces that make up climate and environment.)

TO BREAK A SPELL OF BAD WEATHER, cast a circle and consecrate it with salt and water. Light a yellow candle, invoke the elemental spirits of air, fire, water and earth, and then burn salt in a consecrated censer (or other fire-proof container) in the center of the magick circle.

Witch Bottle Spells

To destroy negativity and evil forces, take a small glass bottle and fill it with needles, pins, nails, crushed stones and pieces of broken colored glass. Add the herbs of rosemary, basil and bay. Seal the bottle tightly with a cork or lid, and then pour melted wax from a white candle over the seal. Hold the bottle in your hands and say:

WITCHES' BOTTLE OF HERBS AND CHARMS
BANISH EVIL AND WARD OFF HARM
PROTECT ME FROM ALL ENEMIES
THIS IS MY WILL. SO MOTE IT BE!

Hide the bottle in a cupboard or bury it at the farthest corner of your property when the moon is waning.

To punish wicked people who have done you harm, or to break the power of an evil hex and turn the black magick back upon the instigator, fill a witch-bottle with old, rusty coffin nails, tacks, black pebbles, broken glass from a mirror burned in fire, deadly nightshade and urine.

Using dragon's blood resin as a Witches' ink, inscribe the name of the person whom the witch-bottle spell is directed at on a piece of parchment and insert it into the vile mixture.

Seal the bottle tightly with a cork or lid, shake it vigorously 13 times and then pour melted wax from a black candle over the seal. Draw a pentagram on the ground and place the bottle in the center of the symbol. Light five black candles and place one at each point of the pentagram. Take your athame in your right hand, hold it over the top of the bottle and say:

AS THIS WITCHES' STAR BURNS BRIGHT
  WITH FIRE
SO SHALL (name of victim) BURN IN MY IRE.
MAY HE/SHE SUFFER TIL I
  SET HIM/HER FREE.
CURSED BE, ENEMY, CURSED BE!

Bury the bottle as close to the front door of the victim's house as possible. As you do this, visualize in your mind the kind of revenge you would like to have upon this person. He or she will be plagued by sickness and misfortune until the time the witch-bottle is unearthed and broken.

This is an extremely powerful revenge spell and it should be carried out only when absolutely necessary.

7

Magick for Hearth and Home

Hearth Magick

The hearth has long been associated with magick, superstition and the occult. To the ancient Romans and Greeks, the hearth was a humble, earthbound temple wherein domestic gods and goddesses dwelt. To honor their household deities, they kept the hearths ablaze with sacred fires that burned day and night.

As the centuries passed, faeries, spirits and goblins

took the place of the ancient deities. Countless superstitions and fantastic folk tales about the hearth and its strange, supernatural inhabitants arose and were passed down from generation to generation.

At one time, many people believed that there were good spirits who lived in the hearth and protected the house and its occupants against thieves, bad spirits and sorcery. When moving from one place to another, a family would always take along the spirit of their house in order to ensure good fortune and continued protection. This was done by taking a burning ember from the grate in the old house and using it to start a fire in the hearth of the new house. This ancient occult custom is where the word "housewarming" originally came from.

To Witches and magicians, the hearth has always been regarded as a very magickal place for it is there that cauldrons filled with mystical ingredients boil and bubble, spells are cast, fire spirits are invoked, fire-scrying and other forms of divination are practiced, and omens of fire, smoke and ashes are interpreted.

The following plants were traditionally burned in Witches' hearths to make the house fragrant, to cast healing spells, and to ward off negativity and disease: angelica root, anise, cloves, coriander, deer tongue, evergreen root, lavender, lemon verbena, lilac blossoms, oak leaves and branches, orris root, rosemary, rose petals, St. John's Wort, violets and wintergreen.

From ancient times to the present, the following magickal herbs and incenses have been burned in hearths to repel ghosts, demons and venoms: angelica, basil, bay, clover, cloves, dill, dragon's blood, fern, frankincense, garlic, horehound, juniper, lilac, mallow, mandrake root, marigold, mint, mistletoe, mugwort, peony root, rue, sandalwood, Solomon's seal, St. John's Wort, thistle, vervain and yarrow.

TO BLESS A HEARTHSTONE IN A NEW HOUSE,
you must first burn six laurel twigs or six leaves from an
oak tree together with some fragrant herbs in a place
other than the new hearth. Take the ashes and mix
them with sea salt. Light three white candles and place
them around the hearth. Sprinkle a handful of the salt-
ash mixture over the hearth and say:

> BY THE POWER OF THE GODDESS
> AND ALL SPIRITS OF THE FIRE
> I NOW CONSECRATE THIS HEARTH.
> BLESSED BE! BLESSED BE!

> MAY ALL FIRES THAT BURN HERE
> FILL THIS HOUSE WITH THE WARMTH
> AND LIGHT OF LOVE, HEALTH,
> AND ETERNAL HAPPINESS.
> SO MOTE IT BE!

TO PREVENT DEMONS FROM ENTERING A
HOUSE THROUGH THE CHIMNEY, many witches in
England as well as New England used white paint or
chalk to draw three magickal ring symbols on the
hearth. The symbol of the ring, like all magick circles, is
a highly potent image, and its use as a powerful shield
against dangerous, hostile forces can be traced back to
many ancient cultures around the world. The shape of
the ring, possessing neither beginning nor end, is symbolic of infinity, perfection and constant renewal. Three
(the number of rings) is a sacred, spiritual and extremely magickal number symbolic of the Triple Goddess (Virgin, Mother, Crone) and the Moon (waxing,
full, waning). White (the color of the rings) is symbolic
of the Mother Goddess and is also the color of purity
and protection.

House Blessing Ritual

One hour before midnight, light white votive candles and place one in every window of the house. Turn off all electric lights, unplug telephones, etc. The entire house should be very quiet and still and all precautions should be taken so that no negative or disturbing outside forces be permitted to interfere with the ritual.

Erect an altar in the center of the house. Place upon it a silver ritual sword, a censer of rose-scented incense, two white altar candles, a small dish of salt and a goblet of white wine. Cast a circle of protection around the altar. Light the candles and incense, and then begin consecration by sprinkling a pinch of salt and a few drops of wine over the sword and censer. As you do this, say:

I CONSECRATE THESE TOOLS OF MAGICK
IN THE DIVINE NAME OF THE GODDESS
BLESSES BE! BLESSED BE!

Begin the blessing ritual at the first bell of midnight, the witching hour. Take the sword in your right hand, the censer of incense in your left hand, face the altar and recite the following prayer of blessing:

IN THE NAME OF THE GODDESS
I BANISH AND EXORCISE FROM THIS HOUSE
ALL MALIGNANT SPIRITS, DEMONS AND IMPS
ALL NEGATIVE AND DESTRUCTIVE VIBRATIONS
AND ANY EVIL INFLUENCES THAT MAY DWELL
WITHIN THIS PLACE.

MAY THIS HOUSE BE FILLED
WITH LOVE AND PEACE.
MAY GOOD LUCK AND FORTUNE
NEVER CEASE.

PROTECTED AND GUARDED
MAY THIS HOUSE BE
CLEANSED AND PURIFIED
OF NEGATIVITY. BLESSED BE!
BLESSED BE!

Hold the sword pointing away from you and slowly move clockwise. As you do this, imagine a glowing white beam of positive energy flowing out from the tip of the sword and being absorbed into the entire room. Continue moving clockwise until three full turns have been made. Move on into the next room with your censer of incense and sword and repeat the prayer of blessing. Continue on into the next room and the next until every room of the house (including the basement, attic and garage) has been blessed and filled with positive energy.

It is important to have incense burning throughout the entire ritual to drive away unseen negative forces and to infuse all rooms of the house with positive vibrations. If the incense should burn itself out at any time during the ritual, relight it or add more rose incense to the censer right away.

Now go outside and stand, facing the front door of the house. Point the sword at the door, visualize energy light flowing, and say:

BLESSED BE THIS HOUSE
AND ALL WHO ENTER HEREIN.
SO MOTE IT BE!

Do this in front of every door leading into the house and then walk clockwise three times around the house, visualizing the entire building completely covered by a protective white light.

To end the rite, return to the altar and give thanks to the Goddess for her love and assistance. Uncast the circle and extinguish the candles.

TO REMOVE BAD LUCK OR CURSES FROM A HOUSE: Take 13 yarrow sticks and burn them in the fireplace at midnight on St. John's Eve (June 22). After the fire has died out, take a consecrated athame in your right hand and draw the Seal of Solomon in the ashes. (The Seal of Solomon is a six-pointed star or hexagram. It is called the "Star of David" by the Jewish people, and in medieval times it was used as an alchemical symbol of the antagonistic elements of fire and water fused together. The triangle pointing up signified fire, and reversed, the triangle signified water. The combination of the two elements represented harmony.)

TO PROTECT A HOUSE AGAINST EVIL AND SOR-CERY: Nail a horseshoe above the front door or tie a stone with a hole in the middle to a white string or gold chain and hang it in a window. Draw or paint seven six-pointed stars (hex symbols) on the door of a house or barn to guard it against wicked spells. Pentagrams (five-pointed stars) painted, drawn or carved onto doors or window shutters are also quite effective.

TO KEEP A KITCHEN SAFE FROM EVIL SPIRITS AND BAD LUCK: Place seashells, onions or a bulb of garlic on the window sill. Hang aloe flowers from the door lintel or hide a witch-bottle in a cupboard. (To make a witch-bottle for the kitchen, fill a glass with nails, pins, needles, avens root, mugwort, salt and red wine. Seal the bottle tightly, shake it nine times and then let some melted wax from a red candle drip onto the cork or lid. Touch the top of the witch-bottle with a consecrated athame, bless it in the name of the Goddess, and then burn some sandalwood incense to seal the spell.

TO PROTECT A HOUSE FROM BEING STRUCK BY LIGHTNING: Scatter ashes across the roof of the house, hang a house-leek from the rafters or nail a sprig of mistletoe above the front door. Hang olive branches on the chimney to keep it safe from lightning or cut St. John's Wort on Midsummer's Eve and hang it in a window.

TO OPEN LOCKED DOORS: Find a *dead* frog and pulverize it into powder. (Never kill a live frog or toad! It will bring you bad luck.) Mix it with a tiny bit of henbane and the milk of a black cow. Let it sit in the sun for three days. It is said that a small amount of this mixture placed in any lock will cause it to open.

TO EXORCISE GHOSTS FROM A HOUSE: Allow sage to rot under a dungheap. This will breed worms which, when thrown into a fire, will make a thunderous noise that will drive out all unwelcomed spirits. Scare away poltergeists by slamming every door in your house three times. An old-fashioned method of exorcism used in 17th century New England to rid houses of mischievous ghosts and hostile Indian spirits is as follows: Light a white candle after sunset on a Sunday. Carry the candle in your right hand and salt in your left hand as you walk backwards through every room of the house, starting in the cellar and working your way up to the attic. As you enter each room, sprinkle some salt and say:

SACRED SALT AND FIRE BURNING BRIGHT
PUT THE IMPIOUS DEMONS TO FLIGHT.
REMOVE ALL EVILNESS FROM THIS PLACE.
LET ALL WICKED GHOSTS SET FORTH IN HASTE.
YE VENOMS MOST FOUL, NOW HEARKEN TO
   ME:
DEPART FORTHWITH AND BANISHED BE.
FLY FAR HENCE AND NE'ER RETURN
OR IN THE PIT OF FIRE I'LL DAMN YE TO BURN.

TO KEEP THIEVES FROM ENTERING YOUR HOUSE: Take a red sachet bag and, by the light of the moon, fill it with a bit of powdered mandrake root, powdered John the Conqueror root, garlic, basil and a small piece of turquoise. Hang the bag above your door to help protect your house from being robbed.

8

Voudoun Candle Magick

Voudoun Candle Magick

Voodoo is a very old and primitive-like system of both black and white magick, deriving from a background of African theology and ceremonialism. It is a complex of Catholic and African religious beliefs and rituals, establishing a vital link between the material world and the world of spirit, and governing in large measure the life of the Haitian peasantry.

The many deities of the Voudoun religion are called *loas*. (Loa is the Congo word for "spirit.") The ultimate purpose of Voodoo is to allow the loas, which possess the strength of nature's forces, to manifest themselves in living human bodies so that the person possessed can be strengthened by drawing on the energy and divine wisdom of the loa.

It is said that when a man or a woman is under possession of a loa, the spirit climbs upon the shoulders of the host in the same manner of a rider mounting a horse.

Each different loa must be worshipped on its own sacred day and "fed" an offering of sacrificed chickens or goats, fruits and other food.

Without the possession of physical bodies and the offerings of sacrificed animals which are traditionally left at crossroads at midnight, the loas would lose their supernatural powers and disappear forever.

There are two major categories of Voudoun deities: the Rada loas and the Petro loas. There are also minor classes of loas and these include the Congo, the Ibo, the Nago and the Wangol. (Voodoo was created in the West Indies by African slaves who had been sold to the slave traders by their African kidnappers and transported to the Caribbean. The slave-trade drew on many different African tribes, each having their own religious practices and beliefs. This explains the reason why Voudoun deities are grouped into separate categories.)

The Rada are protective loas, principally of Dahomean and Nigerian derivation, and invoked mainly in rituals of white magick. (The name Rada is derived from a village in Dahomey called Arada.)

The Petro are aggressive loas that were brought to Haiti in 1768 by a Spanish *houngan* (Voodoo priest) by the name of Don Pedro, who was well known for introducing the practice of drinking rum mixed with finely crushed gunpowder. The Spanish houngan also introduced many new Voodoo rites to the Haitian slaves, including a wild spirit-dance, more violent than the old Rada dances performed by the priests and priestesses of the island. Therefore the Petro cult of black magick and its loas are named after Don Pedro, the "divine messenger" responsible for their worship.

The worship of the loa is directed by the houngans and mambus, the Voudoun priests and priestesses respectively. Using white magick, they can heal people who are sick or injured; using black magick, they can make the dead return to life as zombies to bring trouble or even death to an enemy.

Foretelling the future is another important function of the houngan and mambu, and it is as diviners that they are most often employed. Divining is usually performed while under possession of a loa, but other methods such as crystal-scrying may also be employed.

At a Haitian loa-invoking Voodoo ceremony, *veves* (intricate, symbolic emblems of the various loas to be invoked) are drawn with flour or ashes on the ground of the clearing on which two peristyle sanctuaries (one for the Rada loas and one for the Petro loas) have been erected. In the center of the peristyle stands the poteaumitan, the center pole dedicated to the loa Legba through which the loas arise. The appropriate colored candles for each loa are placed over the *veves* and special prayers, including the Catholic prayers of the Ave Maria and Pater Noster, are recited.

After the prayers are finished, the Voodoo drums begin to beat and a chicken, goat or other animal is sacrificed and then given to a cook who prepares it for the altar of the loa. Special songs are sung to the loas as the drums beat an appropriate rhythm and the invocation begins.

Drums are among the central symbols of Haitian Voodoo. They are considered to be sacred as they are an important element of the loa-invoking ritual.

Drumming has many functions within the Voodoo ritual. Through a combination of rhythms played by sticks, middle and master drums, and a loud iron clapper called an *ogan*, the dancers are able to enter a possession-trance. This is often achieved by the master drummer's manipulation of rhythm and meter, including powerful rhythmic disruptions called *casses*. The percussive dance music is also essential for sustaining the ritual setting after the dancers have become possessed by the loas. It is of the utmost importance that the drummers keep the loas dancing and use special rhythms to send away any uninvited spirits.

At a Voodoo ceremony, devotees possessed by loas may give advice to the troubled and perform the miraculous, such as healing the sick and foretelling events of the future.

Loas of the Voudoun Pantheon

The following list contains the names and descriptions of the principal Rada and Petro loas worshipped in the Voudoun religion.

AGWE
Rada Voodoo sea-god, patron loa of fishermen and sailors and consort of the female loa Erzulie. Agwe is envisaged as a green-eyed half-caste often wearing the uniform of a Naval officer.

AIZAN
Haitian Voodoo loa who lives in water and gives 'his devotees the power to heal and to divine the future.

AYIDA WEDO
Haitian/Dahomean Voodoo loa envisaged as a rainbow-serpent goddess of many colors. She is the consort of the serpent-loa Damballah and is often symbolized by a snake, serpent or dragon.

BARON SAMEDI
Petro Voodoo loa of death and black magick. Ruler of cemeteries, envisaged as a dwarf. His symbol is a black cross on a tomb, the cross draped with a black coat and surmounted with a top hat. He controls the souls of men and women murdered by evil magick. It is said that when he is invoked at midnight, the bizarre and frightening sound of rattling chains is heard as he appears. Baron Samedi is the Petro loa most invoked in Voodoo black magick.

BOSU
Haitian Voodoo loa who inhabits mountains and cemeteries. His sacred color is black.

DAMBALLAH
Rada Voodoo loa known as the Serpent of the Sky, the Father of the Falling Waters, and loa of all spiritual wisdom. Damballah is the consort of Ayida Wedo, the rainbow-serpent loa. He is worshipped and invoked on Thursdays and his sacred color is white.

ERZULIE
Rada Voodoo loa of love, beauty and femininity. Her primary attribute is luxury and she is envisaged as a young, beautiful, wealthy lady wearing many golden rings and necklaces. Her favorite drink is champagne and, like the Virgin Mary, her symbol is a pierced heart. But unlike the Virgin Mary, Erzulie possesses a highly erotic character. She is the consort of both Ogoun, the loa of fire and war, and Agwe, the royal loa of the sea. In her Petro form, she is known as Erzulie Ge-Rouge (Erzulie Red Eyes) and is envisaged as a pale, trembling woman who sobs uncontrollably because no one can love her enough. White and pink are her colors and she is worshipped on her sacred day Friday.

GHEDE
Rada Voodoo loa of death. He is the loa invoked at the close of every Rada ceremony. He dresses in the colorful attire of a clown or court jester and often wears between his legs a giant wooden phallus. He sings dirty songs in a nasal voice and delights in embarrassing people in a sexual way. At Great Ceremonies, black goats are sacrificed to him as an offering as well as the

djakati (chickens with ruffled feathers believed to possess the supernatural ability to locate, dig up and destroy evil magickal charms set against their owners). Ghede is known to have an insatiable hunger, and a person under his possession will eat prodigious amounts of ritual food offered. His sacred day is Saturday and black is his favorite color. Although he is the loa of death, he can also be a great healer. In his Petro form, he is known as Baron Samedi, the Ruler of Cemeteries.

LEGBA (PAPA LEGBA)
Rada Voodoo loa of pathways and crossroads. (In the Voudoun religion, any and all crosses have symbolic meaning.) Originally a Dahomean sun god, Legba is the most important loa, and every Rada ceremony begins with an invocation to him. He is the interpreter of the other loas and he allows them to rise up through a stake (the most important ceremonial object in Voodoo) plunged into the ground. He is the guardian and keeper of the keys that unlock the gate separating the material world from the world of spirit. Legba often appears as a limping, poorly-dressed old peasant, smoking a pipe and walking on a crutch, but he is enormously powerful, and it is said that possession of an entranced devotee by him is extraordinarily violent, causing the person's limbs to be contorted as if crippled and their face to become ancient-looking and weary. In Southern Haiti, male goats and the smallest chick from each hatchling are sacrificed to Legba on his sacred day of Tuesday. In his Petro form, he is known as Carrefour, the Master of the Crossroads.

LOCO (PAPA LOKO DAHOMEY)
Haitian Voodoo loa of healing and spirit of herbs and vegetation who gives healing power to leaves. His sacred color is green.

MARASSA
Mysterious twin Voodoo loas that are divine in strength, but human in behavior. The Marassa are believed to be the parents of the entire human race and are the only loas created directly by God (in the Christian sense). They are envisaged as twin children, and when they possess a devotee at a ceremony, they inspire him or her to behave like a child.

OGOUN
Haitian/Nigerian Rada loa of war and fire who protects his worshippers from bullets or wounds inflicted by weapons. He strengthens his devotees by slapping them and lifting them up into the air. And unlike the other loas, he is invoked with the ceremonial pouring of rum which is then set on fire. Wednesday is his sacred day, a sword is his symbol and red is his favorite color.

SIMBI
A loud and often rambunctious Petro Voodoo loa who is known as the Patron of Magickal Powders. He is believed to inhabit mango and calabash trees. He is worshipped and invoked on his sacred day of Tuesday.

SOBO
Haitian/Dahomean Rada Voodoo loa of thunder and lightning, whose sacred symbol is the ram. The Voudounists believe that Sobo forges sacred thunderstones (pre-Columbian axe heads) by hurling a thunderbolt to the earth, striking a rock outcropping and casting a

stone to the floor of the valley. Before a houngan may touch it with his hands, the thunderstone must lie there for a year and one day.

TI KITA

A powerful and much feared female Petro Voodoo loa associated with the cult of magick and the dead. She "feeds" on pigs and goats, and her sacred color is black.

ZAKA

Haitian Voodoo loa of agriculture. He appears as a peasant wearing a straw hat, smoking a pipe and carrying a machete in his hand.

Voodoo Candles

Candles are important tools in Voodoo magick. Without candles, it would be just about impossible to cast spells or invoke the loas.

Most Voodoo candles are made from tallow, the rendered fat of animals. You may use goat tallow to make your candles (in the tradition of the Haitian Voudounists) as long as you don't mind working with greasy and foul-smelling candles. (Beef tallow is recommended instead, for it makes a harder and slower burning candle with a nice luster and clean odor.)

To make Voodoo candles, first purify the tallow by boiling it in fresh rainwater for 13 minutes. (It is very important that the tallow used be clear-grained, perfectly clean fat.) Remove from heat and let it cool until the fat solidifies on the surface. Lift it off of the cold water and dry it with a clean cloth.

Another method which works equally as well is to boil the tallow for 13 minutes in a solution of alum and saltpeter. (Add ½ pound of alum and ½ pound of saltpeter to the water for every 15 pounds of tallow.) Remove the fat from the water after it has cooled and solidified. Dry with a clean cloth.

To make the candle wicks, take some fine, bleached, not-too-course cotton yarn and either twist it into a cord consisting of four threads, or braid together three threads of the yarn. Dip the wicks into a caustic consisting of two percent boric acid diluted in distilled water to give them the proper degree of flammability. Allow them to dry thoroughly in the sun.

Break up the hardened tallow and put it in a metal pot or other fireproof container. Place the pot in a pan partially filled with water, and then melt down the tallow by heating the water over low heat.

To make colored candles, add pieces of broken wax crayons or dye that is soluble in fat. (Candle dye can be purchased in many candle shops and hobby stores.) You may also stir in perfumes or powdered fragrant herbs to the hot tallow if you wish to make scented candles.

The following list contains the different colors and fragrances associated with each principal Voodoo loa:

Voodoo Loa	Color	Fragrance
Agwe	Blue	Lavender
Aizan	White	Angelica
Ayido Wedo	Blue	Hyacinth
Baron Samedi	Black	Myrrh
Bosu	Black	Apple Blossom
Carrefour	Black	Frankincense
Damballah	White	Lilac Blossom
Erzulie	White/Pink	Rose
Ghede	Black	Myrrh
Legba	Black	Frankincense
Loco	Green	Pine
Ogoun	Red	Cinnamon
Simbi	Red	Patchouly
Sobo	White	St. John's Wort
Ti Kita	Black	Orange Blossom
Zaka	Yellow/Green	Honeysuckle

Cut the wicks to the proper length and then dip them into the melted tallow. After the first dipping, roll the wicks between your fingers to thoroughly incorporate the tallow into them and then pull each wick straight and allow them to harden before dipping again. (The wicks may be tied to a piece of wire or thin wood and used as a dipping frame. This will enable you to dip several candles at the same time. Be sure that the wicks are tied approximately three inches apart on the frame and that they all fit into the pot containing the melted tallow.)

Quickly dip the wicks again into the tallow, taking care that they do not bend, and then allow them to cool and harden before dipping them again. (The idea is to add a layer of tallow each dipping and yet not melt off the previous layers.)

Continue dipping until the candles are of large enough diameter. (It will take between 12 and 15 dippings to make a candle with a bottom end of about three quarters of an inch wide.)

After the dipping process is finished, gently straighten out the candles while they are still soft. With a sharp heated knife, cut off the thick bottom part of each candle where the wax has run down. Place the candles on a glass or marble surface and roll each one smooth with the aid of a wooden board or tray. Finish the candle by shortening the top of the wick.

All Saint's Day Ritual

For spiritual strength and protection against evil loas, perform this ritual at midnight on All Saint's Day (November 1st).

Place seven copper coins in a wooden container with rice, biscuits, cassava, bananas and a white chicken that has been killed and then cooked over an open fire. Place the box at a crossroads, light a white candle and recite the following prayer:

> O GREAT PAPA LEGBA
> MASTER OF THE CROSSROADS
> AND COMMANDER OF THE LOAS,
> IN THIS MIDNIGHT HOUR
> OF ALL SAINT'S DAY
> I BRING THIS OFFERING TO YOU.

Sprinkle a bit of raw rum at each fork of the crossroads and in the center. Lift three bits of earth from the corners of the crossroads and take them home with you. Put them in a plate with some rum that has first been lighted and then extinguished.

Anoint yourself with it and say:

> O GREAT PAPA LEGBA
> IN THE NAME OF THE MASTER
> OF THE CROSSROADS,
> IN THE NAME OF THE MASTER
> OF THE GREAT FORESTS,
> IN THE NAME OF THE MASTER
> OF THE MOUNTAINS AND CEMETERIES,
> I ASK THAT YOU PROTECT ME
> IN ALL THAT I MAY ENCOUNTER
> OF GOOD AND OF EVIL.

Voodoo Love Spell

To make a powerful Voodoo love powder, burn a handful of dried roses on a night when the moon is full and mix the ashes with the powdered skull of a serpent and a pinch of white sand.

On a Friday night (when the power of Erzulie is the most intense), make a small wax doll to symbolize the man or woman from whom you desire love. Mix a small bit of hair, blood or powdered fingernail clippings from the intended lover with the wax to give the doll power. (To make it even stronger, dress it in a piece of fabric obtained from the clothing of the person whom the doll is made to represent.)

After the doll has been made, light a tall, pink candle. Tie a red string around the doll and then sprinkle a bit of the love powder over it and say:

> O ERZULIE, LADY OF LOVE
> LET THIS DOLL BE (name)
> LET HIS/HER HEART BEAT FOR ME
> UNTIL I RELEASE HIM/HER
> FROM THIS SPELL.

Pour some champagne on the ground as a libation to the loa, give thanks to her and then wrap the love doll in a white cloth and keep it safe in a secret place.

To break the love spell, untie the red string from the wax doll to release the lover from the power of Erzulie and then burn the doll in a forest clearing when the moon is waning.

Hoodoo

A hoodoo bag is a small hand-made flannel or animal skin bag, filled with poisonous magickal herbs, human and/or animal bones, graveyard dirt, hair and fingernail clippings, and sewn together with a red piece of thread.

A hoodoo bag is a powerful tool of black magick. It is similar in appearance to a mojo bag, but is used to bring bad luck to its victim, physically injure or even kill them.

A hoodoo doll is a small cloth doll stuffed with the same things as the hoodoo bag and also used for evil and destructive purposes. Unlike a Voodoo doll which must be stuck with pins or nails to be effective, a hoodoo doll works by simply being nailed above or on the door of its intended victiim.

To break the power of a hoodoo and to send it back whence it came, craft this special hoodoo-breaker candle by the light of a full moon: Start by taking an old, used candle of any color except red (red is the color of the candle that brings down a hoodoo curse upon people), removing the wick, and melting the wax in a small pot over a low flame.

After the wax has melted down into liquid form, stir in a pinch of St. John's Wort and 13 drops of blood from the third finger of your left hand. Pour the wax into a candle mold or a small metal can with a wick knotted through a tiny hole in the base of the can and tied at the top end to a knitting needle that has been placed horizontally over the rim of the can. (NOTE: To prevent the wax from seeping through the opening in the base, the can should be placed in an enamel tray of ice cold water before pouring the wax. The cold water will cause any small amount of wax dripping out from the bottom of the hole to solidify almost immediately and stop up the hole completely.)

Remove the candle from the can after it has cooled and hardened completely (about 10 to 12 hours). Cut off the knot beneath the can and then pull firmly at the wick, using the knitting needle which it is tied to as a lever. (If you have any difficulty removing the candle from the can, place it in a pot of boiling water for a few seconds to melt some of the wax and make the candle slide out more easily.)

Draw a circle on the floor or ground, using white paint, chalk or flour. The circle should be about four to five feet wide. Place the candle in the center of the circle, and place the hoodoo bag or doll next to it along with a fireproof clay dish. (IMPORTANT NOTE: It is best to wear a silver coin on a chain around your neck for extra protection before you begin the ritual.) Light the candle with a wooden matchstick and hold the hoodoo bag or hoodoo doll over the candle flame until it catches on fire. Immediately drop it into the fireproof dish and as it burns, recite the following magickal rhyme:

> EVIL HOODOO BE NOW BURNED,
> LET THE EVIL BE RETURNED
> TO THE ONE WHO SENDS THIS CURSE;
> MAY HIS PAIN BE THREE TIMES WORSE.

9

Candle Omens and Superstitions

Candle Omens and Superstitions

BAD LUCK

A drip of wax down the side of a candle at a seance presages bad luck or death to the person nearest to that side.

It is considered unlucky to fall asleep with a candle burning.

"If a candle falls and breaks in two, double trouble will come to you!"

A candle left to burn itself out will bring misfortune.

It is considered unlucky to gaze into a mirror by candlelight, especially on All Hallows Eve.

DEATH

If a candle suddenly goes out by itself, it is an omen of a death in the family.

If a candle flame gutters and causes grease to form in a winding sheet, it is a death omen for whoever is sitting nearest to it.

If a candle flame burns blue, it is an omen of death in the offing.

DREAMS

To dream of a black candle is an omen of death or illness.

To dream of a white candle is an omen of true love.

If a young woman sees two white candles in a dream, it is a sign that she will soon receive a proposal of marriage.

A red candle that appears in a dream symbolizes passion and sexual desire.

To dream of five candles is an omen of love and marriage.

To dream of a candle in a holder is an omen of a happy and prosperous future.

To dream of a candleholder without a candle in it foretells sorrow and misfortune.

GHOSTS AND EVIL SPIRITS

A blue light from a candle is a sign that good spirits are nearby.

A tall straight flame on a candle during a seance is a sign that a spirit is present.

In Ireland, it is an old funeral custom to light 12 candles around a corpse to protect the soul of the deceased from evil forces, for it is believed that ghosts and demons cannot cross into a circle of lighted candles.

Always light candles at moments of birth, marriage and death to ensure that evil spirits are kept at bay during these crucial times.

Light a brown candle on the eve of Candlemas for protection against evil spirits, ghosts and sorcerers.

Place a lighted candle inside a carved-out pumpkin on All Hallows Eve to keep evil spirits and demons away.

GOOD LUCK

In Sicily, fisherman burn ornate candles to their patron saint to obtain blessings and protection.

A bayberry-scented candle burned all the way down will bring "good luck to the home and gold to the pocket."

Kill a moth flitting about a candle flame to bring good luck into your life.

Light a brown candle in each room of your house on Candlemas Eve to attract good luck and keep away bad spirits and negativity.

Light a new white candle in a new house to bring good luck and happiness to the home.

HOLIDAY CANDLES

Candles on a Christmas tree ensure a year of light, warmth and plenty for the family.

Lighting candles in the window at Christmas time originates in the idea that they lit the way for the Holy Family on their way to Bethlehem.

A red candle burned on the eve of Yule ensures prosperity for the coming year.

The traditional lighting of candles on a birthday cake symbolizes good luck and health for the coming year.

A wish will be fulfilled if all the candles on a birthday cake are blown out in one breath.

LOVE AND MARRIAGE

A pink candle burned on Saint Valentine's Day will bring true love.

A burning candle placed in a window will ensure the safe return of a lover.

Accidentally knocking a candle out is a lucky sign that there will be a wedding in the near future.

Light a white candle on your wedding day to ensure a long and happy marriage.

If a candle suddenly goes out by itself during a wedding ceremony, the marriage will surely end in sorrow.

To make a lover come to you, stick two pins through the middle of a red candle at midnight and when the candle burns down to the pins, the lover will arrive.

An old wedding custom in Brittany and Alsace is to light candles before a newlywed couple and the candle that burns out first indicates whether the bride or groom will die first.

To test the fidelity of a lover, according to a rural American custom, light a candle outdoors near his or her house. If the flame burns towards you or your lover's house, your lover is faithful. If not, your lover is faithless.

To reclaim the affections of a lost lover, thrust two pins or needles through the wick of a burning candle as you say out loud the name of your lover.

MONEY

Light a green candle on a night of the new moon to attract money.

To light a candle from the fire will prevent you from ever growing rich.

WEATHER

If a candle will not light, a storm is brewing.

If the flame of a candle gutters and waves in a room where there is no wind or draft, it is an omen that bad weather of some kind is imminent.

If the flame of a candle burns blue, it is a sign of frost.

A blessed candle from a candlemas rite can be used to conjure storms.

MISCELLANEOUS

A candle with a tall straight flame indicates the arrival of a stranger.

A candle showing a bright spark indicates that the person sitting opposite will receive a letter.

According to old French and German beliefs, only a girl who is "pure" can blow back into life a candle that is sputtering and dying.

A Medieval belief was that a lighted candle placed between the horns of a goat could make the devil appear.

According to Slavonic tradition, only a priest can light three candles at the altar. For an ordinary layman to do so would lead to the greatest misfortune.

Churches only used beeswax candles because it was believed that bees came from Paradise.

A lighted candle (the Hand of Glory) positioned between the fingers of a corpse's hand, traditionally a hanged criminal, was believed to possess various magickal powers such as opening locked doors, making the dead speak and freezing people in their footsteps.

10

Resources

The following chapter is an up-to-date alphabetical directory of occult shops and/or mail order businesses that carry an assortment of magickal candles (such as herbal, healing, altar, hand of glory, Voodoo, etc.) as well as other necessary Witchcraft supplies such as ritual tools, robes, herbs, potions, talismans, etc.

ABYSS
34 Cottage Street
Easthampton, MA 01027-1022
(413) 527-8765
Over 2500 titles specializing in Witchcraft, magick, alchemy, Native American and women's studies, to name a few. Also tarot decks, candles, oils, herbs, jewelry, incense, crystals and cards. Current catalogue price: $2.00 (refundable)

ANNWYN TRADESMAN
P.O. Box 321
Atco, NJ 08004
Finely crafted New Age tools, ornaments and works of art. Current catalogue price: $2.50 (includes free Rune sample)

ARADIA BOOKS
P.O. Box 972-G
Burlington, VT 05402
Teachings, resources and tools for the Age of Flowers, focusing on women's spirituality, priestess craft, Goddess studies, earth religion, crystals, positive magick, etc. Current catalogue price: $1.00

ARS OBSCURA
P.O. Box 20695
Seattle, WA 98102-1695
(206) 324-9792
Publisher of Occult classical visual art, reproductions of engravings and wood-cuts to poster format, grimoires, occasional ritual knives and daggers. Current catalogue price: $2.00

BELL, BOOK & CANDLE
5886 Rocky Point
Long Island, NY 11778
Candles, oils, incense, herbs, sachets, pyramids, tarot
cards, Voodoo dolls, books, tapes, etc. Free catalogue.

BLUE EARTH DREAM TRADING CO.
8215 S.E. 13th Avenue
Portland, OR 97202
(503) 231-1146
Shamanistic-oriented tools, smudging herbs, crystals,
feathers, Tibetan bowls, lunar and animal totems, etc.
Current catalogue price: $2.00

CAT CREEK HERBS
P.O. Box 227
Florence, CO 81226
Homemade potpourris, dried flower and herb wreaths,
purification sage smudges, plus other products and
books. Current catalogue price: $1.00

CELTIC FOLKWORKS
RD #4, Box 210, Willow Grove Road
Newfield, N.J. 08344
Celtic folkworks is a family-run business specializing in
traditional Celtic design handcrafts and jewelry. Cur-
rent catalogue price: $1.00

CERES' GARDEN
R#3, Box 305
Alvin, TX 77511
Feminist Witchcraft accessories: silk altar cloths, tarot
wraps and spread cloths, velvet tarot, amulet and crys-
tal bags embroidered in gold and silver with symbols of

184

the Goddess. Herb-filled dream pillows, custom-made necklaces for healing purposes and more. Current catalogue price: $1.00

CHURCH OF ALL WORLDS/NEMETON
2140 Shattuck (#2093)
Berkeley, CA 94704
Triple Goddess and Horned God T-shirt designs, cassettes, Goddess replicas, books and pamphlets. Current catalogue price: $1.00

CHURCH OF UNIVERSAL FORCES
P.O. Box 03195
Columbus, OH 43203
(614) 252-2083
Psychic counseling, readings, Pagan marriages, Magickal, ritual and occult supplies. Correspondence course in Wicca and Voodoo, etc. Current catalogue price: $5.00

COVEN GARDENS
P.O. Box 1064
Boulder, CO 80306
Incense, oils, bath salts, candles, robes, talismans, ritual kits and much more. Current catalogue price: $3.00 (refundable with first purchase)

THE CRYSTAL ROSE
P.O. Box 8416
Minneapolis, MN 55408
(612) 488-3715
Hand-wrapped crystal pendants, gemstone jewelry, magick wands with spell scrolls, amulet bags, runestones, New Age stationery and much more. Send SASE for free catalogue.

CURIOS & CANDLES
289 Divisadero Street
San Francisco, CA 94117
(415) 863-5669 (12:00-6:00 p.m. PST)
A wide selection of items for the metaphysical community, including ritual oils, incense, herbs, books, jewelry and hard-to-find occult items. (No catalogue available)

ENCHANTMENTS
341 East 9th Street
New York, N.Y. 10003
(212) 228-4394
Witchcraft supply store and catalogue. Herbs, Shaman goods, chalices, daggers, incense, books, crystal balls, oils, candles, tarot cards, Wicca study groups, lectures, classes, workshops. Tarot and astrology readings by appointment. Current catalogue price: $2.00

THE EXCELSIOR INCENSE WORKS
P.O. Box 853
San Francisco, CA 94101
(415) 822-9124
Incense from around the world, raw materials to make incense, crystals, religious statues from India, candles and many gift items. Current catalogue price: $1.00

THE FORMULARY
P.O. Box 5455
Grants Pass, OR 97527
Astrologically-correct incenses, bath salts, oils, candles, books, jewelry and many other occult supplies. Current catalogue price: $2.50

GOLDEN ISIS CATALOGUE
P.O. Box 726
Salem, MA 01970
Magick candles, herbs, books, tarot cards, crystals, natal charts and readings. Free catalogue.

GRAY MOUSE MEDICINE BAG CO.
2717 Sudderth Drive
Ruidoso, NM 88345
(505) 257-2717
Medicine bags, crystals, cassette tapes, bead works, fetishes, books, incenses, etc. Current catalogue price: $2.00

ISIS
5701 East Colfax Avenue
Denver, CO 80220
(303) 321-0867
Metaphysical New Age center, candles, books, incense, herbs, jewelry, tapes, crystals, stone pendulums, art works, etc. Current catalogue price: $3.00

JOAN TERESA POWER PRODUCTS CO.
P.O. Box 542
Safety Harbor, FL 34695
Complete spiritual and occult needs: herbs, oils, incense, pure resins, books, etc. Free catalogue.

LLETHTOVAR CREATIONS
P.O. Box 855
Urbana, OH 43078
Images of the archetypal Earth Mother and Her Priestess, hand-carved in stone and available in many stones, styles and sizes. Rainbow necklaces, Minoan

breast beads and amulet bags. Current catalogue price: $1.00

THE MAGIC ATTIC
251 West Central Street (#189)
Natick, MA 01760
Handmade Wiccan products, ritual incense, scented oils, tarot cards, botanicals, unusual Pagan gifts, dream pillows, potpourri, hand-crafted candles, ritual kits, incense burners and much more. Current catalogue price: $2.00

MAGICKAL CHILDE (formerly The Warlock Shop)
35 West 19th Street
New York, N.Y. 10011
(212) 242-7182
Witchcraft and occult supplies. Free catalogue.

THE MAGICKAL MIND
P.O. Box 3737
South Pasadena, CA 91030
(818) 282-7255
Incense, oils, candles, tools for divination and psychological development, books, handmade jewelry, crystals, etc. Current catalogue price: $2.00

MERLIN'S HUT
P.O. Box 219
Galveston, IN 46932
Handmade charms, amulets, talismans, rare artifacts, also psychic readings, a free correspondence course on Witchcraft and a Witchcraft Museum. Current catalogue price: $1.00 and SASE (For most items, our price is WHATEVER YOU CAN AFFORD TO PAY plus the ACTUAL postage!)

MOONDANCE
P.O. Box 593
Varysburg, NY 14167
21 varieties of fragrant stick incense, 48 kinds of oils, handmade earthenware incense burners and other items of interest to magickal folk. Current catalogue price: $1.00

MOONSTAR PSYCHIC & SPIRITUAL CENTER
38422 Lake Shore Blvd.
Willoughby, OH 44094
(216) 942-5652
Candles, books, cards, incense, tapes, herbs, oils, powders, jewelry, crystal balls, etc. Current catalogue price: $2.00

MYSTERIES
9 Monmouth Street
London, WC2, England
Telephone 01-240-3688
The largest store in the U.K. stocking New Age and Occult books and products. Free catalogue.

MYSTIC MOON
4433 Park Blvd. (Dept. D)
San Diego, CA 92116
(619) 543-1070
Wiccan mail order & shop, offering: beeswax candles, books, oils, incense, crystals and much more. Current catalogue price: $1.00

THE OCCULT EMPORIUM
102 North 9th Street
Allentown, PA 18102
(215) 433-3610
All traditional magick, Witchcraft, demonology literature and supplies including special candles, herbs, oils,
books, altar equipment, jewelry, swords, robes, bones,
skulls, etc. Current catalogue price: $2.00

PANPIPES MAGICKAL MARKETPLACE
1641 N. Cahuenga Blvd. (or Box 1352)
Hollywood, CA 90028
(213) 462-7078
Complete line of occult supplies, handmade robes, tarot
pouches, jewelry, books, crystals, hand-blended incenses and oils, etc. Tarot, palmistry and numerology
readings given on premises. Current catalogue price:
$5.00

PAN'S FOREST HERB CO.
411 Ravens Road
Port Townsend, WA 98368
Tarot decks, unique books and bulk herbal tinctures.
Free catalogue.

ROTHSCHILD-BERLIN
2250 East Tropicana, Suite 19
Las Vegas, NV 89119
(702) 795-1902
Collector's catalogue of weird things, mysterious relics
and bizarre artifacts, plus hundreds of hard-to-find occult titles for collectors. Current catolgue price: $5.00

SALAMANDER ARMOURY
15258 Lakeside Street
Sylmar, CA 91342
(818) 362-5339
Hand-forged athames, swords and other ritual tools fashioned to lunar cycles. Send SASE for free catalogue.

SOFT TOUCH
Box 213 (Dept. RC)
Bryn Mawr, CA 92318
Custom candles. You choose size/shape, color/scent. Over 1000 geometric, ritual, figurine and decorative candles. More than 125 scents (or request one of your own) and almost any color. Occult candles (knob/ wishing, witch, skulls, cross, etc.) plus candle burning supplies. Current catalogue price: $2.00 (applied to first order)

TECHNICIANS OF THE SACRED
1317 N. San Fernando Way (Suite 310)
Burbank, CA 91504
Books, music, oils and ritual supplies related to Neo-African systems, Voudoun and ritual magick. Current catalogue price: $5.00

TOUCH STONE
1601A Page Street
San Francisco, CA 94117
(415) 621-2782
Candles, crystals, ritual oils, altar goods, books, incense and other occult items. Current catalogue price: $2.00

THE UNICORN FORGE
105 Crescent Street
Mazomanie, WI 53560
Knives and swords, all manner of metalwork, positive path ONLY. Write, giving specifics including sketches with dimensions where known for prices. All edged tools are forged. All pieces warranteed against defects in materials and workmanship, and cleansed prior to shipping to give owner purest receptacle for charging their needs.

WILLOW KEEP
P.O. Box 664
Wilton, N.H. 03086
(603) 672-0229
Herbs, pathworking tapes, Pagan T-shirts, incense, natural wands, dolls, altar statues, bronze pentacles and more. Also workshops and open rituals. Current catalogue price: $1.00 (refundable with order)

WORLDWIDE CURIO HOUSE
P.O. Box 17095-G
Minneapolis, MN 55417
World's largest Occult, Mystic Arts supply house. Thousands of curios, books, herbs, oils, gifts, unique jewelry, talismans. Items from all over the world. Current catalogue price: $1.00

Index

Ablanathanalba Triangle, 137
Agate, 76, 142
All Saint's Day Ritual, 171
Amber, 76-77, 142
Amethyst, 77, 142
Ankh, 22
Aquamarine, 77, 142
Aquarius, 34, 65, 84, 142, 143
Aries, 34, 64, 142
Autumn Equinox, 33, 89, 114-117

Beeswax candles, 20
Beltane, 33, 89, 93-96
Beltane rushlights, 94
Beryl, 77-78
Bloodstone, 78, 142

Cakes for the Dead, 101
Cancer, 34, 65, 83, 143
Candle Blessing Ritual, 26
Candle-gazing, 15
Candlemas, 33, 89, 90-92
Candles, 13-15; colors, 14, 19, 31-58, 169; consecration, 25-26;

crafting, 17-24, 59-60, 94, 168-170; divination, 15; for healing, 59-60, 64-68; for wish-magick, 15; oils, 27-30; omens and superstitions, 175-180
Capricorn, 34, 64, 65, 84, 142, 143
Carnelian, 78, 142
Cat-shaped candles, 14
Christmas, 118-119
Color vizualization, 69-71
Coral, 78-79, 142
Corn dollies, 97-99
Crescent Moon symbol, 22
Crystals, 72-75; consecration ritual, 74-75; crystal-gazing, 102, 161

Daily colors, 35
Daily meditation candles, 15
Devil-shaped candles, 14
Diamond, 79-80, 142
Don Pedro, 160-161
Druids, 49, 93, 97, 101-102, 118

Easter, 43, 106
Emerald, 80, 142
Evil Eye, 78, 79, 83, 140
Exorcism, 157-158
Eye of Horus, 23

Feast of Pan, 90
Fire-scrying, 15
Foralia, 93
Fluorite, 80

Farnet, 80-81, 142
Gemini, 34, 65, 142
Gemstones, 76-78, 142-143
Goddess oil, 27
Good Luck oil, 28

Halloween, 101-105
Healing herb candles, 59-60
Hearth magick, 151-153
Hearthstone blessing, 153
Hematite, 81
Herb oils, 18-19
Herbs, 59-63, 109
Hex symbols, 156
Holly-King, 109
Hoodoo, 173-174
House blessing ritual, 154-156
House protection spells, 156-158
Human image candles, 14

Imbolc, 90-92
Jack-o'-lanterns, 101
Jade, 81, 142
Jasper, 81-82
Jet, 82

Lady Day, 90-92
Lammas, 33, 89, 97-99
Lammas ritual potpourri, 100
Lapis lazuli, 82, 142
Leo, 34, 65, 85, 142, 143

Libra, 34, 65, 84, 142, 143
Lightning, 157
Litha, 109
Lodestones, 82-83
Love powder, 172
Love spells, 132-135, 172
Lucky birth-charms, 142-143
Lughnasadh, 97-99
Lunar healing ritual, 64-68

Magick, 123-158, 171-174
Magick charm triangles, 137
Magick handbell, 139
Magick symbol candles, 22-24
Malachite, 83, 142
May Day, 93-96
Mistletoe, 118-119
Mojo bags, 140-141
Moon Hare, 106
Moon magick, 125
Moon-shaped candles, 14
Moonstone, 83-84, 142
Mummy-shaped candles, 14

Oak-King, 109
Obsidian, 142
Ochnotinos Triangle, 137
Oimelc, 90-92
Onyx, 84, 143
Opal, 84-85, 143
Ostara, 106

Pagan deities, 36-58, 82, 97, 106, 114, 119
Pearl, 143
Pentagram symbol, 22
Phallic-shaped candles, 14
Pisces, 34, 65, 142
Planetary rulers, 130-131
Prophetic dream spell, 144-145

Red cord spell, 138
Resources, 181-191

Ring symbols, 153
Ruby, 85, 143
Rune candles, 21

Sabbat candle colors, 33
Sagittarius, 34, 65, 143
Samhain, 33, 89, 101-105
Sapphire, 85, 143
Sardonyx, 143
Scorpio, 34, 65, 135, 143
Seal of Solomon, 22, 156
Self-Dedication ritual, 128-129
Seven Knob candles, 15
Skull-shaped candles, 14
Spirit oil, 29
Spring Equinox, 33, 89, 106-108
Summer Solstice, 33, 89, 109-113
Swastika symbol, 23

Tallow candles, 168-170
Taurus, 34, 64, 142
Threefold Law, 127
Thunderstones, 166-167
Topaz, 85, 143
Tourmaline, 86, 143
Treasure spell, 146
Triangle, 23
Triple God, 57
Triple Goddess, 23, 56-57, 83, 103, 153

Turquoise, 86-87, 143

Veves, 23, 161
Virgin Mary, 57, 164
Virgo, 34, 65, 143
Volcano Goddess, 52
Voodoo, 159-174; animal sacrifices, 161, 164-165; loas, 159-167, 169; Voudoun candle magick, 171-174
Voodoo candles, 168-170
Voodoo love spell, 172
Voodoo-Witch oil, 30

Walpurgisnacht, 89
Wax dolls, 172
Weatherworking, 147-148
Wiccan Rede, 126
Willow knot spell, 133
Winter Solstice, 33, 89, 118-121
Witch bottle spells, 149-150, 157
Witch candles, 17-19
Witches' Sabbats, 89-121

Yule, 33, 89, 118-121
Yule log, 118

Zodiac candle colors, 34

About The Author

GERINA DUNWICH was born on December 27th, 1959, under the sign of Capricorn with a Taurus rising. She is a self-dedicated Witch, cat-lover, poet, professional astrologer and student of the Occult arts.

She has written many newspaper and magazine articles and is the author of *Candlelight Spells*. She has appeared on numerous radio talk shows across the United States and Canada, and her Goddess-inspired poetry has been published in many publications including *Circle*, *The Georgian Newsletter*, *The Kindred Spirit*, *Mystic Muse*, *The Poet*, *The White Light* and *Xenomorph*.

She is a member of the American Biographical Institute Board of Advisors, and is listed in a number of reference works including *Who's Who in the East*, *Personalities of America* and *Crossroads: Who's Who of the Magickal Community*.

Gerina lives near Salem, Massachusetts, where she edits and publishes *Golden Isis*, a Wiccan literary journal of mystical poetry and Pagan art.

Free Catalog
of New Age & Occult Books From Carol Publishing Group

For over 30 years, the Citadel Library of the Mystic Arts has been hailed as America's definitive line of works on Wicca and White Magic, Occult Sciences and Personalities, Demonology, Spiritism, Mysticism, Natural Health, Psychic Sciences, Witchcraft, Metaphysics, and Esoterica.

Selected titles include: • The Alexander Technique • Amulets and Talismans • Apparitions and Survival of Death • Astral Projection • At the Heart of Darkness • The Bedside Book of Death • Beyond the Light • The Book of Ceremonial Magic • The Book of Spells, Hexes, and Curses • The Book of the Dead • Buddha and the Gospel of Buddhism • Candlelight Spells • The Candle Magick Workbook • The Case for Reincarnation • Classic Vampire Stories • The Complete Guide to Alternative Cancer Therapies • The Concise Lexicon of the Occult • Cosmic Consciousness • Daily Meditations for Dieters • Deceptions and Myths of the Bible • The Dictionary of Astrology • Dracula Book of Great Horror Stories • Egyptian Magic • Egyptian Religion • An Encyclopedia of Occultism • Encyclopedia of Signs, Omens and Superstitions • The Fairy-Faith in Celtic Countries • From Elsewhere • Future Memory • The Grim Reaper's Book of Days • Gypsy Sorcery and Fortune Telling • A History of Secret Societies • The History of Witchcraft • The Hollow Earth • The Holy Kabbalah • How to Improve Your Psychic Power • How to Interpret Your Dreams From A - Z • How To Make Amulets, Charms and Talismans • Hypnosis • Inner Peace in a 9-5 World • The Kabbalah • Know Your Body Clock • The Lost Language of Symbolism, Vols. 1 & 2 • The Magick of Candle Burning • The Magus • Meaning in Dreams and Dreaming • The Modern Witch's Book of Home Remedies • The Modern Witch's Dreambook • The Modern Witch's Spellbook, 1 & 2 • Moon Madness • Not of This World • Numerology • Our Earth, Our Cure • Out-of-the-Body Experiences • The Pictorial Key to the Tarot • The Practice of Witchcraft Today • Principles of Light and Color • Rituals of Renewal • The Roots of Healing • Satanism • Satanism and Witchcraft • The Secrets of Ancient Witchcraft • Shouting at the Wolf • Strange World • Study and Practice of Astral Projection • The Symbolism of Color • The Talisman Magick Workbook • Tarot Cards • Teachings of Tibetan Yoga • A Treasury of Witchcraft • The Vampire • The Werewolf of Paris • What Happens When You Die • Where the Ghosts Are • The Wicca Book of Days • Wicca Candle Magick • Wicca Craft • The Wicca Garden • Wicca Love Spells • Wicca Sourcebook • Wicca Spellbook • Window To the Past • Witchcraft • Witchcraft, Sorcery, and Superstition • You Are All Sanpaku • Zen Macrobiotic Cooking

Ask for these New Age and Occult books at your bookstore. To order direct or to request a brochure, call 1-800-447-BOOK or send your name and address to Carol Publishing Group, 120 Enterprise Avenue, Dept 1831, Secaucus, NJ 07094.

Prices subject to change; books subject to availability